Confucianism, Democratization, and Human Rights in Taiwan

Confucianism, Democratization, and Human Rights in Taiwan

Joel S. Fetzer and J. Christopher Soper

LEXINGTON BOOKS
Lanham • Boulder • New York • Toronto • Plymouth, UK

Published by Lexington Books
An imprint of The Rowman & Littlefield Publishing Group, Inc.
4501 Forbes Boulevard, Suite 200, Lanham, Maryland 20706
www.rowman.com

Unit A, Whitacre Mews, 26-34 Stannery Street, London SE11 4AB

Copyright © 2013 by Lexington Books
First paperback edition 2014

British Library Cataloguing in Publication Information Available

Library of Congress Cataloging-in-Publication Data

The hardback edition of this book was previously cataloged by the Library of Congress as follows:

Fetzer, Joel S.
  Confucianism, democratization, and human rights in Taiwan / Joel S. Fetzer and J. Christopher Soper.
     pages cm.
  Includes bibliographic references and index.
  1. Confucianism—Taiwan. 2. Democratization—Taiwan. 3. Human rights—Taiwan. I. Soper, Christopher J. II. Title.
  BL1844.T28F48 2012
  299.5'121720951249—dc23

                              2012028546

ISBN 978-0-7391-7300-8 (cloth : alk. paper)
ISBN 978-1-4985-0325-9 (pbk. alk. paper)
ISBN 978-0-7391-7301-5 (electronic)

♾™ The paper used in this publication meets the minimum requirements of American National Standard for Information Sciences—Permanence of Paper for Printed Library Materials, ANSI/NISO Z39.48-1992.

Printed in the United States of America

Lovingly dedicated to Shu-nu Wu (吳劉淑女) and Sheng-Pinn Wu (吳聖聘)

- JSF

to Jane Woodwell, Katharine Soper, and David Soper

- JCS

Contents

Figures

Tables

Abbreviations

BHRD	Bureau of Human Resource Development, Kaohsiung City Government
CCP	Chinese Communist Party (共產黨)
DPP	Democratic Progressive Party (民進黨)
KMT	Kuo Min Tang (國民黨, Wade-Giles transcription), the historically dominant Chinese Nationalist Party in Taiwan
chi^2	chi-squared, a statistical measure of the relationship between two variables
df.	degrees of freedom, a measure of the amount of information used to calculate certain test statistics
N	sample size
NICT	National Institute for Compilation and Translation (國立編譯館), Taipei
NT	New Taiwan Dollars (台幣)
p	probability level in a statistical test; indicates the chance of the result occurring by chance
PAP	People's Action Party, the dominant political organization in Singapore
PRC	People's Republic of China (中華人民共和國), mainland China
r	Pearson's correlation coefficient, a common statistical measure of association between two variables
R^2	coefficient of determination, the amount of variance in the dependent variable that is statistically accounted for by the regression equation
ROC	Republic of China (中華民國), Taiwan
WWII	Second World War
χ^2	see chi^2

Acknowledgments

The genesis of this project is our shared interest in religion and politics. Our previous work on both Islam and politics and on church-state relations convinced us that religion remains a key political variable in the "post-modern" world. After the first author married into a native Taiwanese family and moved to Hong Kong, we began to consider how our insights into politics in Western Europe and North America might apply in the East Asian context. This line of thought led us to the most important belief system in the region, Confucianism, and the related "Asian values" claim that democracy and human rights are incompatible with traditional East Asian culture.

The authors are grateful to the numerous individuals who gave of their time and expertise in interviews for this project. They were generous with their advice, unfailingly courteous, and, in several cases, even hosted us at elegant Chinese banquets. The staff at the Los Angeles Taipei Economic and Cultural Office and their counterparts in Taiwan were indispensible in arranging interviews and setting up logistics. In particular, we would like to thank Paul Chang, Kent Yang, Leo Liu, T. K. Lee, John T. C. Lee, and Derek Hsu for their enthusiastic support of our research. All errors of fact or judgment nonetheless remain the writers' alone.

Elsewhere, several other scholars of Taiwanese politics made useful comments on various chapters and introduced us to other key contacts in the field: T. J. Cheng of the College of William and Mary, Shelley Rigger of Davidson College, Vincent Wei-cheng Wang of the University of Richmond, Kun-hui Ku of National Tsing Hua University, Daniel C. Lynch of the University of Southern California, and Jerry McBeath of the University of Alaska at Fairbanks. We also greatly benefited from the expertise of a handful of specialists in ancient Chinese history and culture: Wm. Theodore de Bary of Columbia University, Paul R. Goldin of the University of Pennyslvania, and Edward Slingerland of the University of British Columbia. Finally, Ken Wald of the University of Florida and Ted Jelen of the University of Nevada, Las Vegas, provided key theoretical insights from the literature on religion and politics. To all, we are most thankful, but we do not want to implicate any of them in our errors.

During fieldwork in Taiwan, Joel's extended family by marriage greatly aided in countless big and small ways from ordering up steaming night-market dinners to babysitting a rambunctious toddler and generally making our time in the country both productive and enjoyable. At the beginning of this project, Joel's parents flew to Hong Kong to make sure everyone was OK and to assume such ancestral duties as late-night diapering. At the very end of our work on this book, Pepperdine alum and 台大 graduate student Brandon Alexander Millan aided our efforts by shipping various research materials back to Malibu after Joel had returned to the States and by obtaining one of the cover photos.

Back in California, Pepperdine University's Vice Provost for Research and Strategic Initiatives, Lee Kats, greatly facilitated fieldwork and research assistance by generously funding us via Seaver endowments and course releases. Social Science colleagues Brian Newman and Candice Ortbals gave helpful advice on particular data and theoretical questions, and "Chaplain of Technology" Chris Low helped us out of innumerable computer snafus. We would also like to thank our two research assistants, Amy Yi-Hsien Wu and Christina Chiung-hua Wu, for transcribing many Mandarin- and Taiwanese-language interviews and helping to translate some of the written Chinese texts.

Portions of this text have been previously published as journal articles and are reprinted with the permission of the copyright holders, Cambridge University Press and the Taiwan Foundation for Democracy. Chapter 2 draws upon Joel S. Fetzer and J. Christopher Soper, 2010, "Confucian Values and Elite Support for Liberal Democracy in Taiwan: The Perils of Priestly Religion," *Politics and Religion* [a Cambridge University Press journal] 3(3):493-517. Chapter 3 is based on Joel S. Fetzer and J. Christopher Soper, 2007, "The Effect of Confucian Values on Support for Democracy and Human Rights in Taiwan," *Taiwan Journal of Democracy* [a publication of the Taiwan Foundation for Democracy] 3(1):143-154 and on Joel S. Fetzer and J. Christopher Soper, 2011, "The Determinants of Public Attitudes toward the Rights of Indigenous Peoples in Taiwan," *Taiwan Journal of Democracy* 7(1):95-114. We are grateful to both of these publishers for their help with this volume.

This book relies upon data from the Asian Barometer, World Values Survey, and TNS Research's indigenous rights survey. While these information sources were of great help, neither the producers nor distributors are responsible for the interpretations and analysis in this monograph.

At Lexington Books, Lenore Lautigar deserves our gratitude for accepting the original draft and then seeing the manuscript through production. We trust that her confidence in us will be repaid in future economic and scholarly success for the press.

Joel is once again grateful to 阿華 and Isaak for loving him and tolerating research-induced international travel and Daddy's general grumpiness and to the believers at Ministerios en Su Presencia for praying for his health and safety. The first author dedicates this book to his in-laws, Peter and Shu-nu Wu, for their graciousness and sense of humor in accepting such a 洋番 into the family and helping him to develop an interest in the Chinese language, the unique political situation of Taiwan, and the culture of Asia more generally. Chris acknowledges his children Katharine and David for periodically taking him away from his work and his wife Jane Woodwell for her continued support for his varied academic interests. More importantly, she has provided love and nurture and remains his best friend after over two decades of life together.

Chapter 1
Confucianism and Democratization in East Asia

My friends, why are you distressed by your master's loss of office? The kingdom has long been without the principles of truth and right; heaven is going to use your master as a bell with its wooden tongue.

Confucius (1971:164), *Analects* (III. xxiv)

Accompanied by very little fanfare but overflowing with symbolic meaning, a seventeen-ton, thirty-one-foot bronze statue of the ancient Chinese sage Confucius appeared on Beijing's Tiananmen Square on the night of January 13, 2011 (Jacobs et al. 2011). That Confucius would share the Square with the embalmed body and fifteen-by-twenty foot portrait of Chairman Mao Zedong was ironic, to say the least. During the Cultural Revolution, Mao had heaped particular scorn on what he deemed to be a backward, "feudal" Confucian tradition that supposedly stood in the way of China becoming a socialist paradise. Mao had therefore ordered the destruction of Confucian texts, temples, and statues throughout the country. By 2011, however, Confucius apparently had been successfully re-educated; the statue marked his re-emergence from the political wilderness. Perhaps Communist Party elites thought that they had rediscovered an ancient ally who could provide an ideological rationale for a polity weaving a delicate balance among capitalist economic principles, consumer culture, and authoritarian political practices. Maybe the appearance of the statue was an attempt to cultivate some "soft power" to go along with China's sudden rise to political and economic prominence. Or possibly it was an implicit recognition by party officials that Communism had failed as a unifying belief system for China and that Confucianism might be made to take its place. Yet three months later, on the night of April 20, the figure mysteriously disappeared from Tiananmen Square just as suddenly as it had appeared. No official word has been offered for why the statue was initially erected, or why it was just as suddenly taken down. It is safe to say that Confucius and the Confucian tradition did not change much between January and April of 2011. What apparently did change was the perception among Chinese political elites about how helpful that tradition could be in their larger social and political efforts to maintain power. Perhaps they concluded that Confucius was "feudal" in his thinking after all. Maybe they decided that the ancient philosopher had little to offer to contemporary issues. Or possibly they discovered that the Confucian tradition had resources to challenge the very economic and political practices that they had hoped it might legitimate.

This vignette demonstrates the political relevance of a Confucian tradition that is more than two thousand five hundred years old. In that time, the words and teachings of Confucius have been used, abused, manipulated, and distorted by political leaders. Most often, the tradition has been used to justify political authoritarianism, but more recently some have asked whether Confucianism is actually more consistent with democratic principles and practices. This book will focus on the role of that tradition in the democratization of the Chinese-speaking island of Taiwan. In just under a decade, from the lifting of martial law in 1987 to the first direct presidential election in 1996, Taiwan transitioned from an authoritarian, one-party state to a multi-party democracy. The economic and political factors that contributed to this remarkable transformation have been examined by a number of scholars (Chao and Myers 1998; Copper 2003; Rigger 2003; Roy 2003). Such accounts have effectively explained the mechanics of how and why political change came to Taiwan, but what is less understood is what role, if any, ideology played in this process. The question that we seek to answer in this book is what part Confucianism played in this political progress.

The related social-scientific literature on democratization is vast (Geddes 2009). While works in this field differ in the causal mechanism highlighted, they share a theoretical focus on the economic and political factors that cause democratization. Some of the seminal thinkers in this area include Seymour Martin Lipset (1959), who argues that modernization causes democracy; Carles Boix (2003), who demonstrates that democracy is more likely in countries where the income distribution is more equal; and Adam Przeworski et al. (2000), who counter that while economic development reduces the likelihood of democratic breakdown, it does not by itself cause democratization. Although this literature has made great strides in helping to explain the multiple factors that cause democratic transitions, these studies are largely silent on how democratization changes and is changed by a state's ideological system. We contend that political development is about more than evolving institutions and political practices; it also encompasses a modification in citizens' beliefs about politics. Old ideologies can adapt to those changes and help shape them, or they can be swept aside. What was the fate of Confucianism as Taiwan democratized, and what will this ideology's destiny in the newly democratic state be?

Much of the debate about Confucianism and democracy has taken place at a theoretical level (e.g., Bell 2006; Chuang 2006; Chen 2007; He 2010); the central focus in that conversation has been about the ideological match between Confucian and liberal-democratic values. However, analyzing the function of Confucianism in Taiwan's democratic transition also raises important empirical questions. In actual fact, what has been the historical role of Confucianism in Taiwan? Do any empirical data from the island suggest that adherence to Confucian values is consistent with support for liberal-democratic ones? We will also enter the theoretical argument in the rest of this chapter, but this book primarily focuses on historical or quantitative analysis. Specifically, we will use interviews with Taiwanese political elites, summaries of public-opinion polls, and content analysis of legislative debates and public school textbooks to uncover Confucianism's historical and contemporary role in Taiwan's political liberalization. Our work is thus distinctive in combining theoretical and empirical approaches and quantitative and qualitative analyses in its investigation of the complex relationship between Confucianism and the state on the "Ilha Formosa."

While our focus in the rest of the book will primarily be on Taiwan, the questions posed and answers provided have tremendous relevance for developments throughout the region. Taiwan has democratized, but countries such as China, Singapore, and Vietnam are not nearly as far along in that process. Given the experiences of Taiwan, is Confucianism likely to contribute to democratization in these other countries or to hinder it? Does Confucianism mainly legitimate authoritarian state actions, as has often been the case historically with the tradition, or can an "alternative" Confucianism challenge political authoritarianism and promotes democratization?

The relationship among Confucianism, political development and some form of democracy has generated much controversy in the last half-century. As we noted earlier, Mao Zedong, or at least some leaders of the Cultural Revolution, tried to eradicate this system of thought as anti-Communist (Gregor and Chang 1979; Schirokauer 1991:368). More recently, Singapore's Lee Kuan Yew (Zakaria 1994; see also Lee 2000) has extolled "Asian values"—a proxy for a particular form of Confucianism—for promoting economic development and political stability but also for limiting the kind of "excessive" personal liberties exercised in the West. But Presidents Kim Dae Jung (1994) of South Korea and Lee Teng-hui (1995) of Taiwan countered that Lee Kuan Yew had misappropriated the Confucian tradition for his own self-interested purposes. It would be easy to claim that this argument said more about the contested nature of politics than it did about any inherent interpretive issues within Confucianism except that a similar theoretical debate about the compatibility of Confucianism and democracy also divides social scientists and political philosophers (Xu and Xiao 1988; Barr 2000; Jacobsen and Bruun 2000; Song 2002; Tan 2004; Bell 2006). Scholars such as Peter Moody (1996), Li Chenyang (1997), Robert Weatherly (1999), Hu Shaohua (2007), and David Elstein (2010) highlight how the traditional Confucian stress on hierarchy, social order, and an individual's duty toward others as well as the absence of any particular notion of individual rights may inhibit the promotion of liberal democracy. Samuel Huntington (1996:108) speaks of the "rejection of individualism and the prevalence of a soft form of authoritarianism or limited forms of democracy" in East Asian societies that are imbued with Confucian values. Michael Freeman (1995), Wm. Theodore de Bary (1998), Joseph Chan (1999), Albert H. Y. Chen (2007), and He Baogang (2010) on the other hand, counter that the Confucian tradition is flexible, that it allows for more than one interpretation, and that it can be used as a basis for democracy and human rights.

It is hardly noteworthy to point out that Confucianism has been manipulated by political leaders and regimes to support authoritarian practices and suppress democratic initiatives. What is less apparent is whether this tendency is endemic to Confucianism. To help us think about answers to this question, we want to turn our attention briefly to the German sociologist Max Weber. Weber's work on religion and Confucianism provides helpful, albeit at times contradictory, answers to the issue of how independent Confucianism, or any other ideology, can be from the state. In a surprising way, his work anticipates the contemporary debate about Confucianism and democracy.

Weber's Theories of Ideology and the State

Max Weber is distinctive among western social theorists of the late nineteenth and early twentieth centuries in that he writes extensively about Confucianism. In that work, Weber offers a perceptive analysis of the complex relations between religious ideas and social and political institutions. What is decisive for Weber is the "theoretical attitude toward the world" (1963:209) taught by different religious and ideological traditions. For "salvation religions," including Judaism, Christianity, and Islam, ethical imperatives stand outside and potentially in judgment of worldly practices. This conflict between divine mandates and the way the world actually operates opens the possibility for "tension with and opposition to the world" (1963:207). Conflict can occur "when a religion is the pariah faith of a group that is excluded from political equality but still believes in the religious prophecies of a divinely appointed restoration of its social level" (1963:228). Or, clashes can ensue whenever a gulf exists between "ethical demand and human shortcoming, consciousness of sin and need for salvation, conduct on earth and compensation in the beyond, religious duty and socio-political reality" (1951:235). Weber's point is that religious traditions that have ethical obligations to a "hidden and supra-mundane God" who is beyond the world will at some point find themselves in a "state of tension with the irrationalities of the world" (1951:227 & 236).

For Weber, however, Confucianism "rejected all doctrines of salvation" (1951:122) and sought instead to accommodate itself to the world. The ethical duties in Confucianism were to be found in this world; they "owed nothing to a supra-mundane God" and those values were "never bound to a sacred cause or an ideal" (1951:236). Instead of an external ethic that might motivate adherents, Confucianism was "only interested in affairs of this world such as it happened to be." Far from the goal of world transformation, the objective for the Confucianism acolyte was "adjustment to the world, to its orders and conventions" (1951:152 & 155).

As a consequence, Confucianism became a conservative, world-affirming ethic which "intentionally left people in their personal relations as naturally grown or given" (1951:240). In an authoritarian, tradition-bound Chinese culture, Confucianism necessarily became the ethic "of a particular social class . . . an elite class the members of which have undergone literary training" (1963:127), while at the same time the tradition "facilitated the taming of the masses" (1951:235). Because Confucian values did not reach beyond the observable world, Confucianism simply lacked the theoretical resources to challenge existing practices. In contemporary parlance, Confucianism in Weber's reading could hardly be expected to challenge pre-existing authoritarian practices, or counter those values with more democratic ones.

However, Weber's argument about the autonomous role of religious ideologies in a social order provides a plausible avenue to challenge his own claims about the restricted role for Confucianism. In his general sociological work, Weber argues that religious values and ideas can shape social behavior. A belief system can motivate human action and under certain circumstance shape the surrounding economic and political institutions. To demonstrate his claim, Weber analyzes a very specific question: why did capitalism develop when and where it did? For Weber, the decisive factor was the formation of a Protestant religious ethic. The Reformation introduced a radically new set of values, including the notion of a personal call from God and worldly asceticism, which proved conducive to capitalism. The fulfillment of one's call from God became "the highest form which the moral activity of the individual assumed" (1958:80). Just as "every legitimate calling" (1958:81) had exactly the same worth in the sight of God, so too did everyone have the same obligation to fulfill God's duties on the earth. For the Protestant, the goal was to remake the world in light of God's ethical demands rather than to accept the world as it was. As Weber notes in a footnote, this calling became a "sort of categorical imperative. Only the glory of God and one's own duty, not human vanity, is the motive for the Puritans" (1958:276).

In practice, this worldly asceticism both validated secular vocations and legitimated the division of labor since it produced "unusually industrious workmen, who clung to their work as to a life purpose willed by God" (1958:177). Weber described this moral justification for worldly activity as "one of the most important results of the Reformation" (1958:81). The ethic encouraged success in the world and the accumulation of wealth, supposedly not as ends in and of themselves, but as a "sign of God's blessing" (1958:172). While it was not intended as a way to promote capitalist development, this religious activity "did its part in building the tremendous cosmos of the modern economic order" (1958:181). The historical accuracy of Weber's theory connecting the rise of capitalism with a Protestant religious ethic is unimportant to us; what matters is his claim that ideas influence the behavior of religious adherents. For Weber, religious doctrines work independently of state demands; they motivate behavior and shape outcomes in ways that have little or nothing to do with state interests. Under certain circumstances, those ideas could even work in ways contrary to state or ruling-class interests.

As we noted above, Weber did not imagine that Confucianism could function in a similar way. We suggest, however, that his treatment of Protestantism and his understanding of how religious doctrines could motivate ethical action in contrast to state interests are more relevant to Confucianism than he himself

imagined. Weber contends that because Confucianism was not a salvation religion, no necessary tension existed between the demands of the tradition and the
practical realities of the world. As a consequence, Confucianism was necessarily
a world-affirming ethic. Weber's treatment of Confucianism and Puritanism as
mutually exclusive types of rational thought bears some consideration. While
each worldview provided a way of life for adherents based on a set of beliefs,
they differed, according to Weber, in that Puritanism was a salvation religion,
while Confucianism was not. Thus, Confucianism as an ideology did not create
tension within the world as Puritanism and potentially all other salvation religions did. Even if one assumes for the sake of argument that Confucianism is
not a salvation religion, tensions could still conceivable arise between the ethical
demands of the Confucian tradition and how the world is actually operating. It
might be possible, therefore, that Weber is right that Confucianism seeks "adjustment to the world," but only if the world is in harmony with Confucian values. The Confucian values of social harmony and social hierarchies might ordi-
narily dictate resignation to the political order of the day, but not if the political
rulers are failing to live up to the ethical obligations that they have to those they
govern. Weber might be right that strictly religious traditions have a greater
ideological capacity for conflicts with the world, but it does not follow that a
non-religious belief system such as Confucianism cannot have them as well.

Related to this critique is Weber's treatment of the Confucianism of his day.
Weber first published his work *The Religion of China* in 1915, just a few years
after Sun Yat-sen officially established the Republic of China (ROC). Sun's
effort to modernize China implicitly included a reformulation of Confucianism
in a more liberal direction, but that trend had hardly taken hold when Weber was
doing his research. He was no doubt right that Confucianism functioned as a
conservative ethic in China at the time that he analyzed it. However, Weber is
guilty of reifying a particular interpretation of Confucianism, one that is bound
up with the way that tradition functioned in late nineteenth-century China. But
traditions change, and Weber more than anyone else understood this phenomenon. Protestantism was an outgrowth of Catholicism, and the numerous Protestant traditions that Weber so carefully analyzed were a product of the Protestant
Reformation. Intuitively, Weber appreciates that there is no such thing as a con-
text-free, historically non-contingent force known as Christianity, or even Protestantism. Both Christianity and its Protestant subculture were shapers of and
shaped by historical circumstances. They developed in ways that no one could
predict, shaped the lives and actions of believers, and brought about political and
economic results no one could have anticipated. But, the same argument can be
made about Confucianism. Weber essentializes a narrow interpretation of Confucianism as a statist ideology, failing to consider that the Confucianism he studied in the early twentieth century was no more insulated from historical
processes, and from change, than was Christianity.

Weber, in short, offers opposing ways of resolving the question of the compatibility of Confucianism and democracy. His treatment of Confucianism as an
historical phenomenon implies that he could not foresee that value system ever
undermining authoritarian practices or legitimating democratic ones. However,

his understanding that ideas change and that those norms and values can powerfully influence political outcomes in new and unpredictable ways suggests that Confucian values could bolster democracy.

Ernst Troeltsch, an early twentieth-century German theologian whose work draws on the sociological insights of Weber, is helpful on this point. Like Weber, Troeltsch focuses on the social and political roles played by religious beliefs. His key contribution is distinguishing between a sect and a church as sociological concepts. For Troeltsch, a sect and a church are not just different institutional forms of the Christian religion; they also have divergent social ethics, doctrines, attitudes toward the world, understandings of the religious tradition, and social classes to which they appeal. The church is world-affirming. It is in "close connection with the . . . development of Society," or an "integral part of the existing social order," and it "utilizes the state and the ruling classes" (1960:221) for its own purposes. The message and ethic of the church is a universal one, and it tries to compel "all members of society to come under its influence and sway" (1960:338). By so doing, the church is able to exert considerable influence on society, but it also becomes "dependent upon the upper classes" (1960:331) and ultimately is as much "dominated by the world" (1960:342) as it dominates the world.

Sects, by contrast, "renounce the idea of dominating the world" (1960:331), aiming instead for personal transformation. They appeal largely to the lower classes who are united by an intense commitment to religious faithfulness, but sects do not "believe that the world could be conquered by human power and effort" (1960:337). They are in no position to shape the values of the larger society, but as a result sects have less need than does a church to make compromises with the state. Troeltsch contends that both church and sect are "based upon fundamental impulses of the Gospel" (1960:342). The Christian tradition, therefore, contains the seeds for either institutional form of religion, based upon how the scriptures are interpreted and on what cultural, political, and social conditions prevail.

Troeltsch's distinction between church and sect holds a number of important implications for Confucianism. In his terminology, Confucianism has functioned exclusively as a church. Its ethic is universal, and it has been closely allied with the existing social order, including the ruling, upper classes. In that position, Confucianism has been able to shape the social order and its values, but it has also had to accommodate itself to a largely conservative ethic and has always been in danger of being dominated by the powerful classes, rather than dominating them. However, Troeltsch does not reify the church type as the essential organizational form for religion. Under certain conditions, sects and a sect-like mentality developed within Christianity. Moreover, most religions seem to develop church and sect forms at various times in their history. We see no reason to think that a transformative, sect-like development is impossible for Confucianism or to believe that, if it developed, it would fail to create a Confucian tradition challenging authoritarian practices and promoting democratic ones.

Finally, Weber's insight that ideas are independently important in shaping social and political outcomes has been used in recent years by political scientists.

Rogers Smith (1988) and Robert Lieberman (2002), among others, have argued persuasively for an autonomous role for normative ideas in accounts of politics. Moreover, both of them note that existing theories of politics, which might do a good job of explaining political outcomes at a given moment in time, have a harder time accounting for long-term political change. Only a focus on the role of ideas, and on the way in which ideas about politics can change, can adequately explain the discontinuities in political development. For the purposes of our book, this insight is relevant because East Asia is experiencing dramatic social and political change. What is yet to be explained is the role ideas are assuming in this transformation.

To explore this question, in this chapter we analyze the role of Confucianism in four East Asian societies: Taiwan, the People's Republic of China (PRC), South Korea, and Singapore. These countries are ideal for our comparative purposes for two reasons. First, as we will demonstrate below, there is widespread adherence to key Confucian values in each of these regions. Consequently, we can analyze the role that this ideology plays in the four societies. Second, the nations differ in their degree of democratization. China and Singapore are authoritarian regimes, while Taiwan and South Korea have an authoritarian past but have made the transition to democracy.[1] This political difference should allow us to see if Confucianism as an ideology has changed with democratization.

The data for this chapter come from public-opinion surveys and documents related to the transmission of Confucianism in the four countries. We particularly focused on Taiwan because it is culturally Chinese, which Korea is not, but also adheres to liberal-democratic norms, which is not the case in China and Singapore. Our investigation indicates that although authoritarian governments found and continue to find many resources in Confucianism to buttress their rule, today's liberal-democratic states in East Asia have begun to create a space for the development of a truly independent Confucianism that is either politically "neutral" or even supportive of democracy and human rights.

Public Opinion on Confucianism and Democracy

Confucianism is a rich and complex tradition that does not easily lend itself to simple definitions. What we seek to measure is a least-common-denominator Confucianism that is true to the tradition but does not predetermine our empirical results by veering in a legalist, anti-democratic direction or by taking on a pro-democratic interpretation such as that offered by Mencius (1970). Focusing on the core Confucian texts *The Analects, The Great Learning,* and *The Doctrine of the Mean,* we will therefore define Confucianism as an ethical system that places primary emphasis on family loyalty, social hierarchies, and social harmony (Yao 2000; Oldstone-Moore 2003; Goldin 2011). These three norms lie at the heart of the "five right relationships" that are universally recognized as the foundation of Confucianism.

To measure these three core values, we used one item each from waves one (2001-2002) and two (2005-2006) of the Asian Barometer.[2] Our family loyalty question was whether "for the sake of the family, the individual should put his [or her] personal interests second." For social hierarchies we used "if there is a quarrel, we should ask an elder to resolve the dispute" in wave one and "being a student one should not question the authority of [one's] teacher" in wave two.[3] Our social harmony item was "when one has a conflict with a neighbor, the best way to deal with it is to accommodate the other person." Our democracy indicator was the sum of two questions about the extent to which our country should be "democratic now" and the degree to which "democracy is suitable for our country."

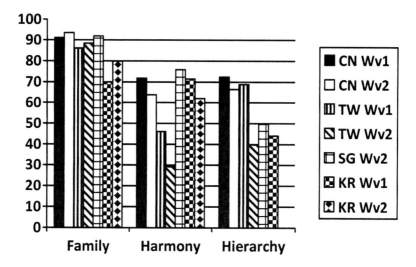

Figure 1.1. Support for Confucian Values in China, Taiwan, Singapore, and Korea (Asian Barometer waves one and two; percent "strongly agree" or "agree").

As figure 1.1 indicates, Confucian values are broadly supported in each of the four countries. If we measure mass-level support, democratization does not appear to have dramatically undermined adherence to these core values. (We interpret the relatively low approval for social harmony in Taiwan as an effect of the deep ethnic tensions between "mainlanders" and "native Taiwanese.") The one variable that might be experiencing a "democratization effect" is that for social hierarchy. In the five years between waves one and two, Taiwanese respondents have reduced their support by 30 percent, and support is also relatively low in democratic South Korea and semi-authoritarian Singapore.

In figure 1.2, we have summarized our bivariate analysis of the correlation between the democracy indicator and the measures of our three Confucian values. In this graph, a negative correlation coefficient indicates that as support for the particular Confucian value rises, enthusiasm for democracy declines. A positive correlation indicates that as agreement with the Confucian value rises, so too does adherence to democracy. In the most authoritarian country, China, all three indicators of Confucianism were associated with lower support for democracy in the first wave. Four years later, however, no Confucian value was negatively correlated with democracy, while one (family loyalty) saw a positive correlation. Substantively, the wave two data may indicate that China's political culture is democratizing even if its political institutions remain rigidly authoritarian. Wave one of these data also confirms Weber's contention that Confucianism in China was a conservative, state-affirming ideology. Our findings are similar for "partly free" Singapore; as enthusiasm for family loyalty and social harmony rise, opposition to democracy increases. However, no statistically significant relationship exists with the third Confucian value, social hierarchy.

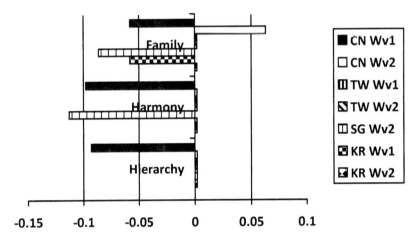

Figure 1.2. Relationship between Support for Democracy and Confucian Values (Asian Barometer waves one and two; Pearson correlation coefficients between democracy and the three Confucian values; r = .002 "stubs" for no relationship).

The results for the two democratic countries, on the other hand, differ markedly from those for the two authoritarian states. In the two waves from Taiwan, no Confucian value has any statistically significant relationship with democracy. Although Confucianism does not yet appear to increase support for democracy, it no longer undermines democratization. The results are similar for South Korea. There, the only Confucian value that inhibits democracy is family loyalty in the first wave. In the second wave, on the other hand, even this correlation had disappeared. These results indicate that as Korea consolidated its democracy, Confucianism became less likely to inhibit democratic values. While the relationship between Confucian values and support for authoritarianism was strong in China and Singapore, this bond appears to have broken in democratic Korea and Taiwan. What could explain this large difference in the role Confucianism plays in authoritarian versus democratic countries?

The Transmission of Confucianism in East Asia

The varying results from the data raise the question of why Confucianism is playing a different role in the authoritarian (China and Singapore) versus democratic states (Taiwan and South Korea). One approach would be to step back causally and examine how people are learning Confucianism in the two sets of countries. Perhaps in authoritarian states, leaders are promoting a Confucian worldview that is consistent with their maintaining political power, and the ideology is assuming the role that Weber imagined for it. In democratic states, however, Confucianism may have become autonomous from the state and begun to develop in ways that Weber could not have predicted. While Weber understood that an ideology could be autonomous from the state, he did not see Confucianism playing that role. But democratic change in the region, along with the separation of Confucianism from the government, might be transforming the tradition in a myriad of ways.

The relationship between the state and Confucianism in China, the first authoritarian state we examine, is long-standing, rich, and varied. For centuries, Confucian thought supplied an ideology that legitimated political authority, it was the basis for the civil-service system used by state officials who exercised power on the emperor's behalf, and Confucianism offered an ethical system that shaped familial and personal values. The cultural and political supremacy of Confucianism was challenged on two fronts in the twentieth century, however. The modernist leaders of the May Fourth Movement of 1919 (Zhou 1960) argued that adherence to Confucianism inhibited political and scientific progress in China, and Mao later attacked it during the Cultural Revolution because it supposedly was "reactionary" and impeded the realization of Communism in China (Rozman 1991; Elman, Duncan, and Ooms 2002).

After some decades in the political wilderness, however, Confucianism has made a stunning comeback in the Middle Kingdom (de Bary 1998; Lynch 2006; Fan 2007; Mooney 2007; Angle 2010). Centers for Confucian studies have been established at a growing number of Chinese universities, books and television programs on Confucianism have become very popular, and Confucius Institutes and language study programs have been formed at universities around the world. None of this activity would have been possible without implicit support from the government, which has at times embraced Confucian values in public statements and proclamations. Significantly, the past two Chinese presidents, Jiang Zemin and Hu Jintao, have promoted, respectively, "rule by virtue" and the creation of a "harmonious society," both of which are widely understood as fundamental Confucian norms. The overseas Confucius Institutes are funded by the government and are part of a larger diplomatic effort by China to promote its "soft power" overseas (Starr 2009). Closer to home, Confucian activities and teaching have begun to appear in the state-run schools, and the government has even allowed for the formation of some private schools that focus on memorization of the classic Confucian texts (Angle 2010).

Some, and possibly much of the popular appeal of Confucianism is that it fills an ideological void left by the decline of any significant belief in Marxism-

Leninism, or Communism, and it offers a value system to counteract some of the harsher features of the newly formed capitalist system. However, it is also hard to avoid the conclusion that the Chinese government's interest in Confucianism is that it helps to legitimate its own rule. While its relevant activities are not as heavy-handed and explicit as the efforts of Lee Kuan Yew in Singapore to justify his political authoritarianism, the Communist Party's interest in Confucianism in China is consistent with its goal of maintaining political power. The brand of Confucianism promoted focuses on personal virtues, Chinese nationalism, and a harmonious society; the government seems to have little interest in advocating a more democratically inclined interpretation of the Confucian tradition. According to our data, at the mass level the government's imprint on Confucianism appeared to have taken hold in the early 2000s; adherence to Confucian values in China was initially associated with lower support for democracy in the first couple of years of the twenty-first century if not several years later.

Our second authoritarian state is Singapore. In the 1980s, the country's founder, Lee Kuan Yew, and his aides set about countering "unwholesome Western influences" by formulating and promoting "Asian values," an allegedly non-ethnocentric way of referring to Confucianism in the island state. According to a 1988 statement by Lee's deputy Goh Chok Tong, economically successful East Asian nations all subscribe to a "Confucian ethic." Goh thus recommended "formalis[ing] our [Confucian] values in a national ideology and then teach[ing] them in schools, workplaces, [and] homes, as our way of life" (Vasil 2004:169-170).[4] Even as early as 1974, however, the ruling People's Action Party (PAP; see Bellows 1970) had already initiated its "Education for Living" and civics curriculum in the secondary schools as a way to foster such "Asian moral values" as filial piety and obedience to the government and other authorities.

Not content with this modest beginning, in 1982 the Ministry of Education asked eight prominent scholars of Confucianism to outline the lesson plans for a new course in "Confucian Ethics." The government then urged ethnic Chinese students, who comprise the majority of pupils in Singapore, to enroll in this Confucianism class instead of one of the other options for fulfilling a new requirement in "religious education" (e.g., Islam, Hinduism, Christianity, or Buddhism). Making explicit the political content of the Confucianism the schools would be teaching, Education Minister Goh Kung Swee asserted that Confucius "believed that unless the government is in the hands of upright men, disaster will befall the country. By the way, the PAP also believes the same thing" (Tan 1989; Kuo 1992; Chua 1995:153-168; Hill and Lian 1995:154-157 & 201-219; Tremewan 1996:91 & 117-119; Rahim 1998:159-183; Hill 2000; Lele 2004). Although some such efforts to force-feed Confucianism later had to be revised in the face of popular resistance and problems with implementation (Wong 1996), one may still conclude that Lee Kuan Yew's state-sponsored "Confucian values" are entirely consistent with the PAP's goal of maintaining its rule (Tremewan 1996).

The Singapore model of the state using Confucianism to legitimate its political dominance is similar to what happened in Taiwan from 1949 until the 1990s, when the Nationalist Party, or Kuomintang (KMT), controlled the island as a one-party state. The party's authoritarian leader Chiang Kai-shek, and to a slightly lesser extent his son, Chiang Ching-kuo, actively promoted Confucianism, and the tradition became a required part of the curriculum in the state-run schools (Gold 1996; King 1996). Not surprisingly, Taiwanese democratic leaders rejected Confucianism, which they associated with the political authoritarianism and cultural imperialism of the KMT, and they turned instead to western, liberal norms to justify their political goals (Fetzer and Soper 2010). The period of one-party KMT rule ended with the 2000 election of President Chen Shui-bian of the Democratic Progressive Party (DPP). Once in power, the DPP reduced the place of Confucianism in the required curriculum and in its stead promoted human rights education (Hwang 2001).

State Confucianism no longer exists in Taiwan; the tradition instead functions as "nothing more than a philosophical-cultural system" (King 1996). A vibrant civil society has emerged in Taiwan which includes multiple organizations offering a wide range of alternative ideological visions (Gold 1996). Many of these groups are explicitly non-Confucian, but others in this new sector include Confucian institutes, think tanks, and private schools to promote the tradition on the island (Wang 2008). The impact of democratization on Confucianism in Taiwan has been varied. On the one hand, popular support for Confucian values may be gradually diminishing. Our data indicate that Taiwanese respondents are less likely than their counterparts in authoritarian states to indicate adherence to two of the three Confucian values (social harmony and social hierarchy). However, the data also show that adherence to Confucian values has no effect on a respondent's support for democracy. It would appear, in short, that the separation of the state from Confucianism in Taiwan has freed the tradition from its association with authoritarian values.

Though Joseon dynastic rulers (Eckert et al. 1990:408-410) and more modern dictators such as Park Chung Hee sporadically attempted to propagate authoritarian Confucian values (Duncan 2002), today's democratic South Korea has largely decoupled Confucianism and the government if not deinstitutionalized the ideology completely. The major "professional Confucianists" in contemporary Korea include academics (e.g., at Sungkyunkwan University's School of Confucian and Oriental Studies) and leaders of Confucian temples or associations, none of whom approximates a "gentry-class" employee of the state in the way that the Confucian scholar-bureaucrat did in ancient China. Though political leaders such as the president might publicly congratulate a new Confucian temple on its opening, the tradition largely survives in the private or voluntary sector. By the end of the military dictatorship, Korean Confucianists argued among themselves "at every election" about whether to "support or attack the regime" and had become "critical of the military origins of the government." Confucian scholars, instead of focusing solely on ordinary citizens' duties to the rulers, began insisting that political leaders follow the "noble man" principle by "lead[ing] exemplary lives before the people." Many pro-democracy activists, moreover, critiqued traditional Confucianism yet "thoroughly mixed" Confucianism and shamanism in their opposition to the authoritarian government. At present, the younger, more politically liberal generation of Confucianists is engaged in a protracted struggle with their more conservative elders over the modern significance of Confucianism in Korea (Kim 1996). Professor of East Asian philosophy Kim Ch'ungnyŏl even goes so far as to argue that early Confucianism is compatible with liberal democracy and may help attenuate the excesses of western capitalism. And former democracy activist and Korean President Kim Dae Jung contended in 1999 that the objects of loyalty and filial piety should be ordinary citizens rather than the authoritarian rulers (Duncan 2002).

In contrast with the situation in Singapore, in South Korea Confucian values "are transmitted not through schools, worship services, or the mass media, but only through spontaneous family indoctrination." According to Korean academic Koh Byong-ik, nothing in the Constitution references Confucianism, and "within the entire school system no part of the curriculum is designed to foster Confucian values and practices." Yet as the traditional Korean family becomes less important, the passing down of Confucianism "also invariably wanes." In short, Korean Confucianism "rarely manifests itself in any organization or institution" but rather subsists simply "in the routines of daily life" and in a relatively "strong family consciousness" (Koh 1996; see also Robinson 1991). Given such a deinstitutionalization of the tradition, one should not be surprised to find little connection between adherence to this ideology and support for democratization.

The data from this chapter suggest several intriguing conclusions about the relationship between Confucianism and democracy. States have often promoted a Confucian ideology that legitimates authoritarian rule, cementing in the minds of many, including Weber, that Confucianism was inherently conservative. In both "Communist" China and anti-Communist Singapore, the state actively propagates a version of Confucianism that is intended to bolster the regime. But, the experience of both South Korea and Taiwan suggests that this relationship is not inherent. In both countries, Confucianism has been decoupled from the state and become a part of civil society, separate from the state. Key Confucian values remain relatively strong in both societies, but the link between those values and political authoritarianism appears to have waned.

Plan of Book

To explore this process in greater detail, we wish to turn our attention now to Taiwan. This island is an ideal place to test the relationship between Confucianism and support for liberal-democratic values. Politically, over the past several decades, Taiwan has evolved into a vibrant, multi-party democracy. Political, women's, and aboriginal rights are well protected in both theory and in practice. The society offers social scientists an unrestricted, transparent research environment. Interviews with Taiwanese political actors can therefore help determine if Confucian values were or are at all important in the political work that political elites do. Confucianism is culturally significant on the island. Elements of the ideology are taught in the schools, the island contains leading centers of Confucian studies, and Confucianism is a key belief system that continues to shape personal attitudes and values (Wang and Li 1999:153-305; Jochim 2003). As is true for most East Asian countries, Confucianism plays a sociocultural role in Taiwan analogous to that of the dominant religion in western states. In this environment, to study religion and politics is to study the relationship between Confucianism and political practice.

In the next section, chapter 2, we test whether or not, in the minds of key political leaders in Taiwan, Confucian values aid or hinder their efforts. The data for the chapter consists of interviews with twenty-seven politicians, democracy or human-rights activists, and journalists in Taiwan. To what extent, if any, do those democratic activists see their efforts as consistent with or contrary to Confucian values? If Confucian values no longer hinder support for democratic values at the mass level, is the same true at the elite level in Taiwan? Chapter 3 focuses on mass-level attitudes toward Confucianism and key democratic values in Taiwan before and after complete democratization. Specifically, we analyze the degree to which Taiwan remained a Confucian society as the country became democratic, and whether or not adherence to Confucian values had any impact on support for democratization, women's rights, freedom of speech, and the rights of indigenous Taiwanese. Chapter 4 examines how the Taiwanese government transmitted Confucian values to young people before and after democratization in the 1990s. In particular, we analyze history, language, and civics textbooks from secondary schools. The question we seek to answer in this chapter is whether or not the teaching, and possibly the perceived meaning, of Confucianism changed as Taiwan democratized. Following the method of our elite interview chapter, chapter 5 similarly analyzes how Republic of China legislators in the Legislative Yuan employed Confucianism in debates over key bills on democratization and our three human rights variables. Finally, chapter 6 synthesizes the findings of the previous chapters and spells out the implications of our results for pro-democracy and human-rights activists in East Asia. In the short run, Confucianism will do little to aid their efforts, but in the long term, as the tradition is decoupled from the state and democracy is consolidated, the ideology can be reformulated in a liberal, democratic way. We thus show how several Taiwanese political theorists and Confucianism scholars have begun to reconceptualize the tradition in a more pro-democratic direction.

Notes

1. According to Freedom House (2009), Taiwan and South Korea are "free," China is "not free," and Singapore is "partly free."

2. Directed and distributed by Hu Fu and Chu Yun-han, the multinational Asian Barometer was produced by the Institute of Political Science, Academia Sinica (Taipei, Taiwan), and the Institute for Advanced Studies of the Humanities and Social Sciences, National Taiwan University, and funded by Taiwan's Ministry of Education, Academia Sinica, and National Taiwan University. Al-

though we are grateful to them for their work, neither the producers nor distributors of these data are responsible for the analysis or interpretations in this book.

3. Unfortunately, the second wave of the Asian Barometer did not contain the same question on social hierarchies. We instead used the best available new question, on the authority of teachers. Moreover, this wave contained no hierarchy measure at all for South Korea.

4. Lee Kuan Yew (2000:488) himself contends that liberal democracy is not appropriate for his country because "Singapore [is] a Confucianist society which places the interests of the community above those of the individual" (no irony apparently intended).

Chapter 2
Confucian Values and Elite Support for Liberal Democracy in Taiwan

If a ruler's words be good, is it not also good that no one oppose them? But if they are not good, and no one opposes them, may there not be expected from this one sentence the ruin of his country?

Confucius (1971:269), *Analects* (XIII.xv)

The Chinese government was livid when the Nobel Prize Committee in 2010 gave its prestigious peace prize to the imprisoned Chinese dissident writer Liu Xiaobo. Liu participated in the 1989 Tiananmen demonstrations and has been jailed on four separate occasions for his human rights activism. His most recent incarceration followed from his involvement in helping to write "Charter 08," a document which calls for more freedom of expression, human rights, and democratic elections, as well as the privatizing of state-owned lands in China. Not surprisingly, China refused to release Liu from prison to receive the award, summoned Norway's ambassador to the Chinese Foreign Ministry for a tongue-lashing, and said that it was an insult for the committee to have given the prize to "a criminal who violated Chinese law." Such behavior was all to be expected, but what followed next was more surprising and creative. A group of Chinese, no doubt with the government's stamp of approval, announced an international competition to compete with the now "discredited" peace prize: the Confucius Peace Prize. Not only would this new award snub the Nobel Committee, but naming it in honor of Confucius would send the message that Chinese values were distinct from western ones (Wong 2011).

When the Chinese selection committee announced that its inaugural award would be given to Lien Chan, however, things got a bit more confusing. As a former chief of the KMT in Taiwan, Lien was no less a politically innocent selection than was Liu for the Nobel Peace Prize. In 2005, Lien had visited China as the head of the KMT to meet with the Chinese President, Hu Jintao. At a press conference after his meeting, Liu announced that the animosity between the Chinese Communist Party (CCP) and the KMT was "a thing of the past, and what is important is to work together to create the future." He further elaborated that the KMT opposed Taiwanese independence and would pursue peaceful stabilization of the Taiwan Strait. Rightly or wrongly, democracy activists in Taiwan interpreted Lien's comments as supporting unification and minimizing human rights. Possibly because of this controversy from his past, Lien quickly distanced himself from the Confucian award, saying that he had never heard of the committee and had no intention of accepting the prize. A year later the Chinese Ministry of Culture announced that the Confucius Prize would be canceled, suggesting, perhaps, that they had learned their lesson: a too heavy-handed attempt to manipulate Confucius could backfire, at least in Taiwan (Hong 2005b).

This story is a vivid reminder that Confucius remains politically and symbolically relevant 2,500 years after his death, and that debates over the meaning of his legacy are another in a long list of tensions in cross-strait politics. The anecdote also underscores the question of the compatibility of Confucianism with liberal-democratic values. The actions of the Chinese government suggest that they wished to send the message that Confucius himself would never have advocated the awarding of a peace prize to a "common criminal." But is this characterization of the meaning of the Confucian tradition as it relates to human rights accurate or fair?

As we noted in the first chapter, debate rages about the compatibility of Confucianism and democracy in East Asia. The results of our analysis suggest that Confucianism is more open to democracy than many imagine and that the tradition may well be transforming itself as countries such as Taiwan and South Korea become more democratic. Support for democracy, however, is more than just adherence to a set of political principles about sovereignty and governmental power. It also includes values and commitments to a set of liberal rights, chief among them being free speech, women's rights, and the rights of minorities. Those who have argued that Confucianism is inherently hostile to democracy have made much the same claim about its capacity to promote those liberal values.

Our first chapter focused on mass-level attitudes toward democracy but was silent on how political elites and democracy activists in actual practice understand the relationship between Confucianism and liberal democracy. The issue in this second chapter is not whether Confucianism theoretically advances a set of political norms, nor if Confucianism at the mass level predicts support for liberal democracy. Rather, our goal is to examine whether political activists, on the ground, see Confucianism as an aid or detriment to their efforts. Do the people involved in the democracy and human-rights movements in Taiwan perceive the Confucian tradition as positive, negative, or neutral in the arguments that they make and in the work that they do? The data for this chapter consist of twenty-seven interviews conducted by the first author in Mandarin or English in Taiwan in May of 2008 (see bibliography for full list of interviewees). We generally selected these people because they are politically influential, not because they are necessarily experts in Confucianism. To the extent that Confucianism as an ideology matters for politics, it should appear in the work of political elites on the ground. The interviewees were also selected on the basis of their involvement with one of the following four issues: democratization, Taiwanese aboriginal rights, women's rights, and freedom of speech or the media.

We chose these four values because they have been articulated as fundamental human rights through international declarations, treaties, and conventions. The first and most important of these statements, the Universal Declaration of Human Rights, affirms in Article 19 that "everyone has the right to freedom of opinion and expression; this right includes freedom to hold opinions without interference and to seek, receive and impart information and ideas through any media and regardless of frontiers." Article 21 of the same treaty states that "everyone has the right to take part in the government of his [or her] country, directly or through freely chosen representatives" and that "the will of the people shall be the basis of the authority of government; this will shall be expressed in periodic and genuine elections which shall be by universal and equal suffrage and shall be held by secret vote or by equivalent free voting procedures" (United Nations 1948). In a similar way, the United Nations' (2008) Declaration on the Rights of Indigenous Peoples affirms that "indigenous peoples are equal to all other peoples, while recognizing the right of all peoples to be different, to consider themselves different, and to be respected as such." Finally, the United Nations' (1979) Convention on the Elimination of all Forms of Discrimination against Women recognizes the "dignity and worth of the human person and . . . in the equal rights of men and women." While these norms are not without controversy and interpretive debate, they have nonetheless become the basis by which the international community defines individual, gender, group, and political rights.

Our interviews also allow us to see if Confucianism is becoming more amenable to democratic values over time. Or in Weberian terms, is the ideology shaping political values and transforming itself into a sect-like movement that can challenge authoritarian practices? As we noted in the first chapter, this change seems to be occurring at the mass level in the democratic countries of South Korea and Taiwan. Is a similar process under way at the elite level, where an authoritarian Confucianism once held sway? This chapter opens with a brief history of the democracy movement in Taiwan. Following this account, we offer an interpretation of the Confucian texts on the four political variables that we highlight throughout the book: democratization, indigenous people's rights, women's rights, and press freedoms. We find that Confucianism offers competing narratives on these political values; depending on how one reads the tradition, Confucianism can either be an aid or a hindrance to the promotion of these principles. What is less open to interpretation is how democracy activists understood their political involvement. Our interviews with former and contemporary democracy and human-rights activists thus uncover the role they believe Confucianism has played in their activities.

Chapter 2

Political History of Taiwan

Taiwan's history is replete with powerful outsiders controlling and manipulating the island. Over the past several centuries, Taiwan has been taken over by the Spanish, the Dutch, the Manchus, the French, and the Japanese, who ruled the island from 1895 until the end of World War II in 1945. The Republic of China gained control of Taiwan at the war's end, but four years later the ROC army, President Chiang Kai-shek, the political leadership of the Kuomintang, and 1.3 million refugees retreated to Taiwan in defeat at the hands of Mao Zedong and the People's Liberation Army. In 1949, the KMT imposed martial law on the island, and this status remained in effect for nearly forty years. During that time, the government banned opposition parties, restricted press freedom, and prohibited the formation of autonomous civic associations (Copper 2003:29-66; Roy 2003:76-104; Chang and Chu 2008; Taylor 2009).

Besides trying to dominate the island politically, the KMT attempted to impose cultural uniformity on a population that was linguistically and ethnically diverse. In practice, this policy meant the establishment of Mandarin Chinese, which a majority of Taiwanese could not speak, as the island's official language and the development of an educational curriculum intended to develop a Chinese consciousness among the native-born Taiwanese population (Chen 2004:31-46; Lynch 2006:160). The educational program promoted Chinese history, culture, and language, and either ignored or rejected a Taiwanese consideration of these topics. Crucially for our purposes, the KMT also embarked on a self-conscious effort to include Confucianism in the curriculum. When Mao embarked on his Cultural Revolution that included an outright rejection of the Confucian tradition and religion in general (Marsh 2011), Chiang Kai-shek countered with the Chinese Cultural Renaissance Movement, which introduced students to a conservative, moralistic Confucianism that was clearly intended to promote public support for the regime (Moody 1998:85-90).

Despite its authoritarian practices, the KMT developed the island economically (Gold 1986; Cheng 2001) and brought to Taiwan ideological principles and constitutional arrangements that contained democratic elements. The party promoted Sun Yat-sen's Three Principles of the People (nationalism, popular sovereignty, and economic justice), but claimed that a period of tutelage was needed until Taiwan was ready for democratic self-rule. The government also held local assembly elections, and while these elections were tightly controlled, Shelley Rigger (1999) notes that they nevertheless had a liberalizing effect. The contests created expectations for fairer future elections, and they served as a catalyst for the opposition to mobilize and challenge the regime over its failure to live up to its own stated principles. Among the key moments in Taiwan's eventual democratization were the lifting of martial law in 1987, the pro-democracy "Month of March" student protests in 1990 (Wright 2001; Lee 2004; Chang and Chiu 2005:II:104-109; Millan and Fetzer 2008), the first reelection of the National Assembly in 1991, the elections for the Legislative Yuan in 1992, the first direct, popular election of President Lee Teng-hui in 1996, and the election of the opposition Democratic Progressive Party (DPP) presidential party candidate, Chen Shui-bian, in 2000 (Chu and Lin 2001; Rigger 2001; Chang et al. 2004; Blundell 2012).

Today, roughly 98 percent of the island's population is "Han Chinese," with the other 2 percent consisting of indigenous people divided into 14 recognized groups (*China Post* 2009). However, the "Han" on the island remain deeply divided between "mainlanders"/waishengren [外省人], those who emigrated from China in 1949 and their descendents (currently 14 percent of the population), and "native Taiwanese"/benshengren [本省人]/cai-te-lang [在地人], those whose ancestors typically arrived well before 1949 (84 percent of the population). Part of this ethnic resentment is rooted in the inter-communal violence unleashed during the February 28 Massacre [二二八] of 1947, in which thousands of Han residents of the island—including much of the native-Taiwanese elite—lost their lives at the hands of enraged civilians or the KMT army (Durdin 1947; Kerr 1965; Lai, Myers, and Wei 1991).

Democratization and Confucianism

Virtually all analysts recognize that the close identification of Confucianism with the state historically provided a rationale for authoritarian political elites to manipulate the tradition for their purposes (but see Nan 2004:95). As Brooke Ackerly (2005:557) has noted: "State Confucianism became the practice of deference to authority by bureaucrats. . . . In this sense Confucianism was institutionalized in authoritarian rule." Where scholars differ, of course, is whether the historical implementation of Confucianism exhausts what the tradition theoretically offers to democratization. Wm. Theodore de Bary (1998:154) contends that Confucius "emphasized the benefits of free political discussion and open criticism of those in power," concepts that would allow for such key democratic practices as freedom of speech and assembly. Speaking specifically of Taiwan, Huang Chün-chie and Wu Kuang-ming (1994:79-80) suggest that "there is no more fertile soil than Taiwan to facilitate" the democratic potential within Confucianism.

The debates about the compatibility of Confucianism and democracy reflect the diversity of interpretations that are possible from reading three of the foundational Confucian texts (*Analects, The Great Learning,* and *The Doctrine of the Mean*).[1] Many of the passages from these works seem to provide for a fairly rigid and hierarchical political structure. Frequently, Confucius likens the affairs of state to those of the family, at one point affirming in *The Great Learning* (ix) that "the ruler, without going beyond his family, completes the lessons of the state" (1971:370). Those lessons, of course, are filial piety and fraternal submission. If the government is like a family, then by analogy just as the son is deferential to his father and the younger brother submits to his elder kin, the governed must respect the wishes and guidance of their political "betters." In the *Analects* (I.ii), the philosopher Yu is quoted on a similar point (1971:138-139):

> [T]hey are few who, being filial and fraternal, are fond of offending against their superiors. There have been none, who, not liking to offend against their superiors have been fond of stirring up confusion. . . . [F]ilial piety and fraternal submission! Are they not the root of all benevolent actions?

For the governed, virtuous behavior therefore consists of not stirring up confusion by questioning the authority of political superiors. The relations between "superiors and inferiors," Confucius (1971:258-259) notes, is "like that between the wind and the grass. The grass must bend, when the wind blows across it" (*Analects*, XII.xix).

A common theme throughout these works is that natural hierarchies exist and that good government follows from recognizing and accommodating this chain of political command. When asked at one point about government, Confucius (1971:256) replied: "There is government, when the prince is prince, and the minister is minister; when the father is father, and the son is son" (*Analects*, XII.xi). Good government, in short, is a function of people understanding their proper role in society and fulfilling the functions appropriate to their status. "The superior man," Confucius (1971:395) notes in *The Doctrine of the Mean* (xiv), "does what is proper to the situation in which he is; he does not desire to go beyond this. In a position of wealth and honor, he does what is proper to a position of wealth and honor. In a poor and lowly position, he does what is proper to a poor and low position." The social and political status quo is set, almost preordained, and only disorder can ensue if the relevant classes forget their proper place. Finally, in *The Doctrine of the Mean* (xx) Confucius (1971:409) paternalistically likens a ruler to a parent cultivating the virtues of his children: "By dealing with the mass of people as his children, they are led to exhort one another to what is good." Natural hierarchies, political paternalism, meek acquiescence to the political order of the day, and the obligation of the governed to respect and follow the wishes of their rulers are hardly the stuff of democratic politics. Given these themes, it is not hard to see how a conservative, political authoritarianism became so dominant within the Confucian tradition. However, that understanding is but one reading of Confucius on politics.

While Confucius consistently promotes the existence of natural hierarchies, he is even more insistent on the mutual reciprocity in the obligations that bind rulers and those they govern. In the *Analects* (XIII.vi), Confucius (1971:266) suggests that "when a prince's personal conduct is correct, his government is effective without the issuing of orders. If his personal conduct is not correct, he may issue orders, but they will not be followed." Not only does this quotation emphasize the importance of virtue in a political leader, but it also suggests that people will disobey rulers whose conduct is not admirable. This passage therefore implies that a leader has to earn political legitimacy through his just actions. The virtuous behavior by which to judge a ruler, moreover, is his capacity to serve the needs of the people. When asked by Duke Ai how to win the "submission of the people," Confucius (1971:152) replies, "advance the upright and set aside the crooked, then the people will submit. Advance the crooked and set aside the upright, then the people will not submit" (*Analects* II.xix). A leader without good qualities, in short, does not deserve the support of the people.

The very democratic idea that political legitimacy can only be won by the active support of the people who are governed is even more pronounced in a lengthy exchange between Confucius (1971:254) and one of his disciples (*Analects* XII.vii):

> Tsze-kung asked about government. The Master said, "the requisites of government are that there be sufficiency of food, sufficiency of military equipment, and the confidence of the people in their ruler." Tsze-kung said, "If it cannot be helped, and one of these must be dispensed with, which of the three should be foregone first?" "The military equipment," said the Master. Tsze-kung again asked, "If it cannot be helped, and one of the remaining two must be dispensed with, which of them should be foregone?" The Master answered, "Part with the food. From of old, death has been the lot of all men; but if the people have no faith in their rulers, there is no standing for the State."

To suggest that the ruler can do nothing without the support of the people is a deeply democratic idea. Similarly, *The Great Learning* (x) admonishes that "by gaining the people, the kingdom is gained, and by losing the people, the kingdom is lost" (1971:375). While Confucius might have promoted the inevitability of political hierarchies, then, he also provided a basis for critiquing the state and a foundation for democratic legitimacy.

A passage later in the *Analects* (XIII.xv) even suggests that people have a moral obligation to oppose bad rulers: "If a ruler's words be good, is it not also good that no one oppose them? But if they are not good, and no one opposes them, may there not be expected from this one sentence the ruin of his country?" (1971:269). Criticism of a leader who is failing in his ethical obligations to the people, in short, is essential. Finally, while it is apparent that Confucius divided the world into groups of people with established roles, it does not follow that he imagined those hierarchies to be forever fixed. In short, there is very little evidence from any of the texts that Confucius had in mind some notion of a divine right of kings that flowed from family ties. Instead, hierarchies were a function of the skills and attributes that individuals possessed, and those abilities could presumably be nurtured in virtually anyone. The way to develop those characteristics, of course, was through education (1971:313-314; *Analects* XVI.vii):

> Those who are born with the possession of knowledge are the highest class of men. Those who learn, and so, readily, get possession of knowledge, are the next. Those who are dull and stupid, and yet compass the learning, are another class next to those. As to those who are dull and stupid and yet do not learn, they are the lowest of all people.

By birth, people have different attributes—some have more knowledge than others—but presumably the naturally gifted come from all classes of society. Moreover, this passage implies that the desire and capacity to gain knowledge (and thus move up the hierarchy) is open to anyone who wishes to obtain it. In the end, then, a different interpretation of the Confucian tradition can highlight the very democratic ideas that rulers owe much to their subjects, that political legitimacy rests ultimately with the people, that subjects have a moral obligation to oppose bad rulers, and that social and political hierarchies are not firmly established.

So how has the Confucian tradition been received and interpreted by pro-democracy activists in Taiwan? Our interviews with democracy leaders suggest that Confucian values had little or nothing to do with the movement's political goals. Peng Ming-min (2008), a former DPP presidential candidate and long-time democracy activist, put it succinctly when he noted to us: "We in the democracy movement based our ideas on western thinking. I don't personally think that there is a relationship between Confucian thinking or teaching and western democracy. The starting point for the democracy movement in Taiwan was western notions of human rights and freedom of speech." Several other interviewees juxtaposed the Confucian moral tradition with the more rights-based legal system of the modern world. While conservative values made sense in an ancient context, these respondents suggested, such norms cannot be the basis for a democratic culture. Though acknowledging the positive values Confucianism espouses, Tsai Chi-hsun (2008), Secretary General of the Taiwan Association for Human Rights, nonetheless contended that laws, not Confucian morals, need to be the basis for human rights:

> Rights are traced back to the Constitution, which is a contract between the country and the people. The safeguards for our rights are the laws formulated by legislatures on the basis of the Constitution. Of course, morals and ethics are important, but I think that laws are the foundation of a truly democratic state.

Echoing such arguments, Tim Wu (2008), Director General of Kaohsiung City Government's Bureau of Human Resource Development (BHRD), contrasts the needs of the past with those of the present:

> In the past we had a culture of obedience and loyalty, and we had a philosophy of personal and family discipline. In that context, what does transparency or neutrality mean? To be neutral is to go against nature. You would be considered disloyal if you were perfectly neutral. But a democratic culture needs to have civil servants and administrators who are politically neutral. This prevents political abuse and being contaminated by partisan influence. In the past you just needed to show your loyalty to your emperor, and you were a good person because you were willing to die for him and sacrifice for him. But democratic discipline is different.

In the minds of many of the people that we interviewed, therefore, Confucianism was at best irrelevant in their struggle for political freedom and the rule of law.

The identification of Confucianism with the KMT and the conservative, at times repressive political status quo, poisoned the well for many democracy activists in Taiwan about the compatibility of Confucianism with liberal-democratic norms. As Daniel Lynch has noted (2006), Taiwanese democracy activists self-consciously defined themselves in opposition to the KMT and the "Chinese" identity it sought to impose on the island's aboriginal and native Taiwanese populations. To the extent that the KMT included Confucianism in this effort to shape the Taiwanese cultural experience, it was natural that leaders within the democracy movement would look elsewhere for ideological support for their efforts. Tim Wu (2008; see also Yu 2008) hinted as much to us when he said: "I wrote a book on democracy [Wu 2005] because I wanted to clarify for the Taiwanese people what democratic values [are], how they can be implemented, and how they are different from Confucian values." Looking to western values and away from Confucian ones, in short, was a way for Taiwanese activists to demonstrate their break with the KMT and mainland China.

After the DPP took power, it reduced the amount of time devoted to Confucianism in the public schools and gave greater consideration to specifically Taiwanese history and culture. Liu Jeng-ming (2008; see also Miao 2008), Principal of the Taipei Municipal Zhongzheng Senior High School, noted this change in emphasis: "In the past, more than half of the work in history or geography would be on Chinese history, geography, and Confucianism. Now, there is more of an emphasis on Taiwanese history and geography." This change in emphasis had two important effects. First, it allowed the DPP self-consciously to distinguish Taiwanese from Chinese identity in its educational curriculum, and second, the change implicitly associated Confucianism with the cultural imperialism of the KMT. To democracy activists, then, Confucianism represented everything that they did not like about the political authoritarianism of the KMT.

To the extent that they acknowledge the importance of Confucian values in Taiwanese society, democracy advocates contend that the tradition teaches personal morality that is only tangentially related to democratic principles and practices. Lee Teng-hui (2008), former President of the Republic of China, suggested in our interview with him that "Confucianism teaches about the relationships between people—the five lun (倫)—which can be used to explain how to be moral and to grow personally. It teaches people how to live well . . . but it did not teach us [Taiwanese] how to promote ourselves or to become democratic." Confucian values might still be relevant for personal relationships, Lee implies, but beyond this cultural role the tradition has little to offer in the way of a justification for democracy.

Indigenous Rights and Confucianism

Little or nothing has been written on how Confucianism would theoretically approach the rights of indigenous peoples. Several passages from the *Analects*, however, do speak to the status of minorities more generally. Interpreted literally, there is very little in those texts to suggest that Confucianism would support the rights of ethnic minorities. On at least four occasions, Confucius refers to barbarous people or tribes who do not practice the virtues of a more "civilized" society. The most direct reference comes from the *Analects* (IX.xiii): "The Master was wishing to go and live among the nine wild tribes of the east. Someone said, 'They are rude. How can you do such a thing?' The Master said, 'If a superior man dwelt among them, what rudeness would there be?'" (1971:221). The world Confucius seems to describe is one where superior people and cultures should live, missionary-like, among those that are inferior so that the former can educate the latter. But, the onus is also on those who are inferior to recognize the superiority of those who have come to live among them: "If remoter people are not submissive, all the influences of civil culture and virtue are to be cultivated to attract them to be so; and when they have been so attracted, they must be made contented and tranquil" (1971:309; *Analects* XVI.i). Finally, in *The Great Learning* (x) Confucius suggests that bad, uncivilized people deserve to be punished by being exiled to live with barbarous tribes, who are presumably also uncivilized: "it is only the virtuous man who can send away such a [bad] man and banish him, driving him out among the barbarous tribes around, determined not to dwell along with him in the Middle Kingdom" (1971:378). Moreover, strong historical reasons exist for thinking that Confucianism would be inhospitable to the rights of indigenous people. The ethnic majority Han Chinese have in the past been the ones who primarily interpreted and taught the Confucian tradition. Their identification of Confucianism with Han ethnicity might mean that political activists who support the rights of the non-Han, indigenous Taiwanese do not perceive the tradition as sympathetic to their concerns.

As with democracy, however, some textual resources within the Confucian tradition offer a different view on the rights of minorities, even if these passages are admittedly fewer than was the case for democracy. We noted in our discussion of democracy, for example, that the hierarchies Confucius described were not in his view forever fixed. The capacity to gain knowledge, wisdom, and discernment was learned, and could presumably be acquired by anyone. That assumption was precisely the idea behind exposing "barbarians" to the practices of a more "civilized" culture. Clearly, cultural imperialism lies behind such an idea, which is hardly the basis for genuine respect for indigenous groups, but at least it confirms that the people in those tribes are fundamentally capable of the same level of ethical behavior as the more "superior" cultures. Moreover, various passages in the *Analects* (XVII.ii) imagine people as inherently equal: "The Master said, 'By nature, men are nearly alike; by practice, they get to be wide apart'" (1971:318). The idea that people are born equal is, of course, a basic premise of both democracy and the rights of minorities. While it might not be easy to read into Confucius the contemporary idea that native cultures should be celebrated on their own terms, it is not necessarily a stretch to suggest that he can be interpreted to advance the idea that the people within those cultures are a priori on par with those who are not. He Baogang (2004), for example, has persuasively argued that Confucianism can support the rights of ethnic minorities. Specifically, he contends that the Confucian emphasis on cultural unity and harmony leads to a "Confucian communitarianism" where the rights and values of minority groups are both respected and promoted. The majority may well promote the assimilation of minority groups to Confucian norms, but only in a context that values harmonious relations between the majority and the minority, even to the point of recognizing the validity of group claims. If this reading of the tradition is correct, therefore, political elites belonging to cultural minority groups might come to see Confucianism as an aid in their political efforts.

Today, recognition of the rights of groups, particularly those whose cultures have been severely compromised over the past several centuries, has become a key value in the worldwide democracy movement. Indigenous people (known as Yuanzhumin [原住民] in Mandarin) represent about 2 percent of Taiwan's population. For centuries, these peoples have experienced economic competition and military conflict with a series of colonizers. Government policies under the KMT, particularly in the 1950s and 1960s, actively sought to foster the cultural assimilation of aboriginal people. The use of Mandarin in public schools, an educational curriculum steeped in pro-KMT ideology, and the promotion of Chinese culture and history at the expense of any consideration of native cultures helped to speed the disappearance of a number of indigenous languages and promoted discrimination against indigenous Taiwanese (Kung 2000).

Over the past decade, the government has become much more sympathetic to the political rights of aborigines. In 1996, the Council of Indigenous Peoples was promoted to a ministry-level rank within the Executive Yuan. Beginning in 1998, the curriculum in Taiwan's public schools was changed to give more treatment to aborigines. A minimum of six seats are reserved for indigenous representatives in the Legislative Yuan. In 2005, the Legislative Yuan passed the Aboriginal Basic Law, which guarantees the autonomy of the nation's indigenous peoples and provides government resources for the development of a self-governing system for aboriginal groups (Hong 2005a; Adams 2008; see also Lin 2001). In promoting the "subsistence and development of inter-ethnic relations based on co-existence," the Aboriginal Basic Law marked a decisive break from the assimilation policies of the past. Finally, the former DPP administration supported efforts by the United Nations to implement the Declaration on the Rights of Indigenous Peoples (Calivat Gadu 2008; see also Fan 2007).

According to the interviews we conducted with persons active in the aboriginal-rights movement, Confucian values and the Confucian tradition have hindered their efforts. Kung Wen-chi (2008), an aboriginal member of the Legislative Yuan from the KMT, boldly stated: "Confucius said that people who were different (racially or ethnically) from the Han Chinese should be taught to become civilized and not to be so barbaric. I think that Confucianism is a kind of Chinese racism. It is a hindrance to the aboriginal movement."[2] The Director of the Council of Indigenous Peoples, Calivat Gadu (2008), echoed this sentiment: "most of the aboriginal bills were submitted by indigenous people themselves rather than by Han Chinese, who did not comprehend the needs of Yuanzhumin." When asked specifically about the role of Confucianism in the promotion of those bills, the Director simply concluded that "legislators did not view the issue from the point of view of Confucianism." Pasuya Poiconu (2008), Director of the National Museum of Prehistory and a scholar of Chinese literature, however, is not quite so pessimistic in his assessment of Confucianism. Instead, he draws a distinction between what the tradition theoretically teaches and its political application in Taiwan: "the philosophy of Confucianism doesn't necessarily impede aboriginal rights; the real issue has been the people who have made use of Confucianism to go against the rights of aborigines. In the past, many politicians just wanted to assimilate the aborigines and they used Confucianism to justify that." Kung was even more specific in noting the key role historically played by *his own party* in this process of assimilation: "The KMT came to Taiwan with a conqueror mentality; they had no idea that there was a minority group already living here. They used the Chinese language and culture to get everyone to assimilate. The indigenous people suffered from the dominant ideology of Confucianism as it was put into practice by the KMT government."

As with democratization, the persons most active in the aboriginal rights movement perceive the Confucian tradition as contrary to their purposes. And also as with democratization, one reason for this animosity is the history of the KMT defending its assimilation policies on Confucian grounds. What seems just as significant, however, is the idea of some aboriginal activists that Confucianism is itself a form of cultural imperialism. Seen in this light, it is natural that aborigines would defend their views largely in "western" rather than Confucian terms. The recent initiatives toward state recognition of indigenous peoples are understood as a decisive break from the Confucian, imperialist past and toward a "western," pluralistic future.

Women's Rights and Confucianism

Nothing in the *Analects*, *The Great Learning*, or *The Doctrine of the Mean* explicitly promotes gender equality. Even as staunch and persuasive a defender of Confucianism as Wm. Theodore de Bary (1998:156) has questioned whether the Confucian record on the treatment of women provides any opportunity to make a case for western notions of gender rights. What little discourse exists about women in these documents suggests that Confucius held a traditional opinion about gender roles. In the *Analects* (XVII.xxv), for example, the Master is quoted as saying "Of all the people, girls and servants are the most difficult to behave to. If you are familiar with them, they lose their humility. If you maintain a reserve towards them, they are discontented" (1971:330). In likening women to servants, Confucius seems to suggest that women are morally inferior to men. At best, Confucius promoted a kind of cult of domesticity where women ruled the home and performed the vital, but very traditional, roles of wife and mother. In the home, mothers trained children in the virtues of good citizenship: "This girl is going to her husband's house. She will rightly order her household. Let the household be rightly ordered, and then the people of the State may be taught" (1971:372; *The Great Learning* ix). As vital as that domestic pedagogical role might be, however, the presumption is that gender segregation and female seclusion in the domestic realm are the ideal.

As with the rights of minorities, a literal interpretation of the Confucian texts offers little support for gender equality. However, a less literal reading[3] that highlights key Confucian values can be meaningfully used to support the rights of women. Chief among these is equality, which is an idea actively promoted throughout the documents. For Confucius (1971:318), "men" are by nature "nearly alike" (*Analects* XVII.ii). He consistently rejected the idea that people are naturally born into a status position; instead they earn that distinction through their education and virtuous behavior. While Confucius himself might not have been able to imagine women becoming those persons of distinction, the logical implication of his commitment to equality suggests that there was no reason that they could not. What mattered for Confucius, presumably, was not a person's gender but her or his education and ethical practices. Some contemporary Chinese thinkers have also developed what Doris Chang (2009:9) has described as a "relational feminism" that combines equality with the Confucian idea of distinct gender roles. Men and women might well have particular functions to perform in the family, but those roles are complementary and do not imply the inferiority of women to men.

It is also important to note that what one mostly gets from a close reading of Confucius on the status of women is silence. It is a subject that is hardly touched on at all in any of the foundational documents. The rigid sexism and institutional discrimination against women that developed in East Asia after his death was more a product of the Confucian tradition, and in particular the Neo-Confucianism of the Song Dynasty, than it was a necessary byproduct of what Confucius himself actually taught about the role and status of women (Yao 2000:183; Chang 2009:6).

Prior to the Song Dynasty (960-1279 C.E.), women enjoyed a relatively high social status in Chinese culture, participated in the larger economy, and had a certain degree of freedom outside of the home (Chang 2009:6-8). Song-era Neo-Confucianism reified gender segregation and actively promoted the idea that the only proper roles for women were good mothers and faithful wives and daughters-in-law. This interpretation of Confucianism effectively locked women in an inferior social position for nearly a millennium. Girls were denied access to education, trained only in household management, cloistered in the domestic sphere, and utterly beholden to male relatives or a husband for economic security. Those few girls who were educated were barred from taking the civil service examinations that were required to enter the elite bureaucracy. Moreover, the crippling practice of footbinding (which was ironically intended to mark the distinctiveness of Chinese girls from their "barbarian" counterparts whose feet were unbound) became widespread.

It was not until the nineteenth century that Chinese reformers, borrowing largely from western notions of liberal rights, began to question some of these gender practices. Educational reforms were introduced which allowed women to attend schools, although the number of girls and women in school was minuscule compared to that of boys and men during the early decades of the twentieth century. In 1912 Sun Yat-sen ordered a national ban on footbinding in China. The promotion of gender rights in China became highly complex after the Nationalists abandoned the mainland for Taiwan in 1949. At least rhetorically, the Chinese Communist Party advocated some forms of economic independence and political participation for women (Ackerly and Li 2008). The reality was more mixed, however, but laws were passed that—at least on paper—granted women rights equal to those of men.

Women's movements had emerged in Taiwan during the Japanese occupation under the leadership of pioneering women such as Hsu Shih-hsien (許世賢; Chi 2007). The KMT occupation of the island led to an uneasy co-existence between Chiang Kai-shek's moral and political conservatism and the liberal, western-oriented feminism of most women's groups in Taiwan. Chiang initiated a cultural movement that was conservative, authoritarian, and paternalistic. The Confucianism that he advocated looked very much like the Neo-Confucianism of the Song Dynasty in its promotion of traditional gender roles. Nonetheless, his own wife, Madame Chiang Kai-shek, was hardly a model of female, domestic passivity, and in fact women made great strides in educational attainment throughout Chiang's rule. The Taiwanese women's movement became progressively more active at the same time that the island was democratizing during the 1980s and 1990s (Zimmermann 1987; Chou, Clark, and Clark 1990; Wang 1999; Hsu 2001; Chen Man-Li 2008; Kao 2008). Eventually, their political influence increased enough to allow them to pass such landmark gender-related legislation as the 2002 Gender Equality in Employment Act and the 2000 revisions to the Republic of China Constitution. This latter amendment provided that "The State shall protect the dignity of women, safe-guard their personal safety, eliminate sexual discrimination, and further substan-tive gender equality" (Government Information Office 2009:532).

Given the anti-women legacy of the Neo-Confucian tradition, it is not particularly surprising that the people most active on issues of women's rights in Taiwan uniformly reject the idea that the Confucian tradition, or Confucianism as an ideology, aids their effort. Fan Yun (2008; see also Fan 2004), Assistant Professor of Sociology at National Taiwan University and Director of the Awakening Foundation, one of Taiwan's leading women's rights organizations, suggested the contrast between women's rights and Confucianism when she said: "family values are still very important in Confucianism, and while the women's rights movement is hardly opposed to family values, the family values of Confucianism are based on a patriarchal order that violates the very idea of gender equality." Tzou Jiing-wen (2008; see also Zimmermann 1987:51), Deputy Editor-in-Chief of the *Liberty Times/Ziyou shibao* [自由時報], was even blunter in her assessment: "In terms of the relationship between Confucianism and women's rights, we have to disregard Confucianism completely. I simply don't accept that there is a positive relationship between Confucianism and women's rights." Finally, Lin Fuxiong (2008; see also Huang Shuisheng 2008), a nonpartisan Linzhang from the Zhongzheng district of Taipei, specifically noted the supposed difference between "old" Confucian values and "new" women's-rights norms: "Confucianism is old and not for contemporary society. Today in Taiwan we have gender equality."

Lin is certainly right that Taiwan now has gender equality, or at least much more than in the past. The culturally conservative vision of the unreformed KMT offered little in the way of gender rights. Instead, the party promoted traditional gender roles which were personified in legal codes that gave priority to husbands over wives in custody and property disputes. The democratization movement over the past several decades has dramatically changed the legal and political landscape for Taiwanese women. The government established the Women's Rights Promotion Committee under the Executive Yuan, city governments allocated budgets for women's services, and women's groups successfully lobbied the government to revise the legal code in a more equitable direction. After a nearly decade-long effort, in 2002 the government passed the Gender Equality in Employment Act, which laid an important foundation for women's rights (Ko 2002). The Democratic Progressive Party has been particularly active in courting voters on gender issues. Under DPP president Chen, the number of women in the cabinet increased to one-fourth of the total membership, 30 percent of the DPP seats in the Legislative Yuan were held by women, and Annette Lu [呂秀蓮] became Taiwan's first female Vice President in 2000. Following the DPP's crushing electoral defeat in 2008, for the first time one of Taiwan's major parties nominated a woman as chairperson, DPP-leader Tsai Ing-wen [蔡英文]. As was true for democratization and aboriginal rights, the women's rights movement thus generally sees itself in opposition to the authoritarian and paternalistic legacy both of the martial-law-era KMT and of Confucianism.

Press Freedom and Confucianism

For understandable reasons, the *Analects* contains nothing about restrictions on the media. Arguably, its emphasis on harmonious relations might tend to suppress individuals' willingness to speak out on various controversial issues. In response to a question about whether a "superior man has his hatreds," the Master replies, "He hates the man who, being in a low position, slanders his superiors" (1971:329-330; *Analects* XVII.xxiv). One reading of this passage might be that harmony should take precedence over a person's desire to criticize authority figures. On the other hand, as we noted above, Confucius (1971:269) seems to argue for a duty to oppose bad rulers: "But if [rulers' words] are not good, and no one opposes them, may there not be expected . . . the ruin of his country?" (*Analects* XIII.xv). This duty is precisely what a free press should do in a liberal democracy.

The imposition of martial law in Taiwan severely restricted press freedom and limited the protection of basic human rights. By definition, martial law meant that the government could, and often did, curtail press rights, arrest people for publishing articles that were viewed as critical of the government, and impose severe limitations on the most basic political and human rights. In 1968, the journalist Bo Yang, who had escaped to Taiwan from mainland China because of his opposition to Communism, was arrested and eventually sentenced to nine years in prison for having "mistranslated" the American comic strip *Popeye*. KMT authorities viewed his Chinese rendition of the strip as a veiled attack on Chiang Kai-shek (Bo 1992:xi-xiii). The pro-democracy magazines *Formosa* [美麗島] and *The Eighties* [八十年代], in particular, pushed the limits of what the KMT authorities would allow (Li 2002:132-134). As part of the infamous Kaohsiung Incident, the police closed down *Formosa* magazine and clashed with demonstrators advocating for human rights on the island. Following the demonstrations and violence, the KMT arrested virtually all well-known opposition leaders, charged them with trying to overthrow the government, tried many of them in a special military court, and sentenced them to terms of twelve years to life. Future Taiwan President Chen Shui-bian was one of the defense lawyers in the case, while eventual DPP Vice President Annette Lu was sentenced to twelve years in prison (Landler 2000; Copper 2003:22-23; Roy 2003:160-174: Chang and Chiu 2005:I:76-96). In 1989, Cheng Nan-jung [鄭南榕], the editor and founder of the weekly *Freedom Era* [自由時代] burned himself to death to protest continued restrictions on press freedoms (Li 2002:142-144; Roy 2003:175-176).

The lifting of martial law in 1987 eventually led to a relaxation on press restrictions, to the point that for a time Taiwan had as vibrant and free a press as anywhere in the world. In terms of both press freedoms and human rights more generally, Freedom House rated Taiwan as among the most free nations in Asia. According to Freedom House (2008; Central News Agency 2008), Taiwan rates a 1 in civil liberties (on a scale of 1-7, with 1 being the highest). However, since the inauguration of Ma Ying-jeou in May of 2008 and his subsequent détente with the People's Republic of China, both domestic and international observers have complained about new restrictions on press freedom (Loa 2009; *Taipei Times* 2009).

As with women's rights, those most directly involved in free-press and human-rights issues in Taiwan perceive no link between their activism and Confucian values. Yang Gin-Huey (2008; see also Chen Yi-Wen 2008; Huang Yi Jun 2008), from Amnesty International of Taiwan, specifically contrasts what she perceives to be western, individual values with Confucian, collectivist ones: "compared to Confucianism, human rights emphasize individualism more than collectivism. Confucius talked about the duties that feudal rulers had to emperors, and how they had to follow them. Human rights, by contrast, highlight the rights of each individual person." Kuo Chen-Lung (2008), Deputy Editor-in-Chief of the *China Times* similarly distinguishes what he thinks is the moral authoritarianism implicit in Confucianism with the aggressive journalistic ethic he sees as part of the western tradition:

> In Confucianism the political leader is supposed to be the moral standard for all of us. In that case, it is very hard for him to have room for external criticism. He has to examine himself constantly, but this kind of examination is not the western system that comes from the outside. The independence of journalism, and its role in the system of checks and balances, is not something that comes from Confucianism.

Finally, newspaper editor Tzou Jiing-wen (2008) makes explicit what the others had hinted at: "in terms of freedom of speech and press, we totally disregard Confucian values. If we wish to pursue a better society, we have to get rid of Confucianism so that we can get different opinions and expressions from the people."

It is quite possible that Yang, Kuo, and Tzou are simply wrong in their interpretation of Confucianism; the tradition can certainly be understood as allowing, even challenging, political leaders and established elites and protecting basic human rights, but those most involved in free-press and human-rights issues do not understand the tradition this way. For various reasons, they have concluded that the Confucian tradition of respect for authority and its emphasis on community over personal rights is antithetical to their political objectives.

Elite Rejection of "Chinese" Confucianism

Several conclusions follow from our interviews with Taiwanese elites. First, Taiwanese political activists almost uniformly reject the notion that Confucian values were historically important in the democracy movement or that they are valuable in making a case for liberal democracy in contemporary politics. For many, the Confucian tradition is simply irrelevant. Yang Gin-Huey (2008) of Amnesty International suggested this irrelevance when she said:

> To ask about the relationship between Confucianism and human rights is like asking someone who lived in the feudal era whether they liked the idea of globalization. Or it would be like asking my deceased grandfather whether it is moral to have human cloning. In neither case would it have been possible to imagine such a thing.

Former Chia-yi major Chang Po-Ya likewise (2008; 2012) concluded, "Confucius has nothing to do with advocating for women's rights." The same claim of the irrelevance of Confucianism is apparent in the work of mainland-Chinese democracy activists. In 2008, more than two thousand Chinese citizens living in the People's Republic signed the pro-democracy manifesto *Charter 08* (Zhang et al. 2008; China Charter 08 2009). Our reading of the English translation suggests that the document is based almost exclusively on western, liberal political thought; the original Chinese text itself, meanwhile, appears devoid of references to Confucianism.[4]

A second conclusion is that history explains why the leaders of the democracy movement in Taiwan turned away from the Confucian tradition. Specifically, pro-democracy elites identified Confucianism with the political authoritarianism and cultural imperialism of the pre-democratic KMT, and that identification proved a poison pill for Confucianism. Daniel Lynch (2006) argues persuasively that Taiwanese democracy activists embraced liberal global norms and values as a way self-consciously to distance themselves from what they perceived as the KMT's imposition of a Chinese identity. The cultural and political imperialism the Taiwanese experienced came not from "the West," as was so often the case for other Asian societies, but instead from mainland China. A similar dynamic seems to be at work in this chapter's opening vignette about Liu Xiaobo's winning of the Nobel Peace Prize and the PRC's efforts to establish a competing "Confucius Peace Prize."

Activists in Taiwan interpreted the state-supported Confucianism of the KMT as little more than cultural imperialism and the exercise of naked political power. The KMT's effort to distinguish itself from the PRC by supporting Confucianism, however, had a reverse effect for many Taiwanese activists.

Many such "Tangwai" dissidents rejected the political visions of both the PRC and the KMT, and turned instead to an open embrace of "western" political values. As Huang and Wu have argued (1994), for Taiwanese activists Confucianism became a "problem" to be overcome on the road to political liberalization. This situation helps to explain why the DPP, once it took power, sought to excise Confucianism from the public-school curriculum. A Chinese language teacher responsible for teaching about Confucianism in the high school noted the following irony: "China is now promoting the New Confucianism because of its experience during the Cultural Revolution, which was a revolt against Confucianism and traditional Chinese values. In Taiwan, by contrast, there has actually been a reduction in recent years in the amount of time given to teaching Confucian values in the schools" (Miao 2008).

A related logic leads Taiwanese activists to reject the so-called Asian-values thesis, whether it comes from Lee Kwan Yew or the political leadership of the Republic of China. Chen Mingyu (2008), a Chinese language teacher at Tapei Municipal Zhongzheng Senior High School and someone with a vested interest in promoting Confucianism, had this to say about Singapore's Lee: "Confucianism has historically been misused by rulers. I completely disagree with Lee Kwan Yew. He is simply wrong to say that democratization and human rights do not fit in with Confucianism." As her colleague noted, there has also been a well-documented revival of Confucianism in mainland China, which has used state money to fund "Confucius Institutes" and whose political leaders have publicly promoted selective Confucian values (Fan 2007; Delury 2008; Makeham 2008). Several of our interviewees noted this trend. Rightly or wrongly, however, it seems inevitable that Taiwanese democracy activists will interpret this revival the same way that they have come to understand similar efforts by the KMT decades earlier: as an effort to promote Chinese identity, rationalize authoritarian political practices, and justify limits on individual rights. As Wm. Theodore de Bary (1998:164) has suggested about this Confucian revival, "it can hardly be doubted that Confucianism (or what goes for it) . . . has become the claimed ideological justification for one-party rule, for openly rejecting peaceful evolution to democracy, and for suppressing demonstrations." The adoption of Confucian values in Taiwan is once again caught up in larger geopolitical issues; in this case Confucianism is perceived as a Trojan horse for the People's Republic of China with its desire to annex the island (Shirk 2007:181-211; Wang 2007; see also Taiwan Advocates 2003:23-36; Chi 2004).

In the Weberian terms that we established in the first chapter, democracy activists in Taiwan have come to see Confucianism as an ideology that is inherently authoritarian and incapable of being used to promote liberal-democratic practices and values. But, their understanding of Confucianism is deeply colored by their political experiences. A goodly percentage of our interviewees were members of or sympathetic to the DPP. Some of them personally suffered under the harsh rule of the KMT. Those who are younger in the democracy movement feel the same disaffection with the PRC, which is proffering a kind of Confucianism eerily similar to that the KMT promoted in the 1950s and 1960s. Given this background, it is hardly surprising that political elites active in the democracy movement in Taiwan would discard a tradition embraced by their political opponents.

The role of Confucianism in Taiwan is in many ways analogous to that of the Roman Catholic Church in revolutionary France or Mexico. In each case, democratic or radical reformers self-consciously defined their aims as targeting the primary religious or ideological tradition, which was associated with their authoritarian political opponents and with the dominant power structure. Taiwanese democracy activists might not have been as overt in their "anti-clericalism" as their French counterparts, but only because Confucianism in the late twentieth century was not as institutionalized in Taiwan as Roman Catholicism was in eighteenth-century France. Nonetheless, the effect was the same: political reformers rejected the religion or ideology on the ground that it stood in the way of political progress. As a result, a new kind of nationalism emerged that, in France and Mexico, decoupled national and religious identity, and in Taiwan is trying to do the same for national and Confucian values. Democratic elites in Taiwan thus perceive Confucianism as a fixed, unchangeable ideological bulwark for authoritarianism, much as Weber himself understood the tradition. But as we have pointed out throughout this chapter, that view is not the only way to understand and interpret the Confucian tradition. Weber's appreciation that under the right set of conditions ideas are amenable to change can be usefully applied to Confucian ideology. Democratic elites in Taiwan might see the tradition as forever fixed, but it remains to be seen whether ordinary Taiwanese citizens also view Confucianism as inherently anti-democratic. Or have mass-level respondents found a way to conjoin the two in a way that the elites have not?

Notes

1. Chuang (2006) engages in a similarly close analysis of the classic Confucian texts and generally agrees with our overall conclusion that Confucianism has not necessarily aided political freedom in the past but could be transformed to support human rights in the future.

2. Such attitudes might partly explain—at least at a subconscious level—why indigenous Taiwanese are much more likely to embrace Christianity instead of traditional Chinese religion (Chiu 1997:58-70).

3. Although Legge translates "nüzi [女子]" as "girls" in the main text of the *Analects,* he notes in a corresponding footnote that the term "does not mean women generally, but girls, i.e., concubines." Though this view of even simply "secondary wives" remains sexist, it does not appear to condemn the entire gender. Read in this light, Confucius' comments seem more of a commentary on a sexist system of "domestic politics" than a wholesale critique of all women.

4. Though the English translation of the Chinese phrase "dajia gongzhi, heping gongsheng [大家共治，和平共生]" describes the wording as "traditional Chinese political" thought, the original Chinese-language version of the

manifesto contains only the phrase itself, without this descriptive tag. A fairly thorough search of the Chinese-language versions of the standard Confucian texts also failed to locate this Chinese expression.

Chapter 3
The Effect of Confucian Values on Public Support for Democratization and Human Rights in Taiwan

The traditional culture of China has conferred upon the Chinese a wide range of unseemly characteristics. . . . The political and social system engendered by Chinese-style feudalism was so contrary to every notion of human rights, that one could say that there was no such thing as human rights in China.

Taiwanese journalist and democracy activist Bo Yang (1992:10 & 49)

There is thus no basis for asserting any inherent incompatibility between Confucianism and the human rights to which nations subscribe.

American Sinologist Wm. Theodore de Bary (1998:155)

When EVA Airways (2005), Taiwan's second largest airline, was recruiting flight attendants for its service to Thailand, it required that applicants be fluent in either English or Thai and have a TOEFL score above 450, and it noted that knowledge of Mandarin or Taiwanese would be an added bonus. What was a little more jarring, at least given gender values of the West and increasingly in Taiwan itself, was that applicants had to be female, single and under twenty-four years of age. Moreover, prospective employees had to have a "pleasant personality and appearance with a clear complexion." Apparently as a way to demonstrate that applicants met the necessary requirements, the advertisement asked that two recent full-length color photos be included with the written application. This account about EVA Airways reflects the worse assumptions about one particular issue, gender rights, and Confucianism. Though no direct link exists between Confucian values and the sexist attitudes in the advertisement, anyone reading the story while living in a Confucian society would understand the implicit connection between them. This chapter aims to analyze the link between liberal-democratic values and Confucianism in Taiwan. The previous chapter looked at this question at the elite level; here, we examine mass attitudes.

While political leaders and theorists extensively debate this question, far fewer quantitative studies have measured the relationship between these variables. Three that do include Chang, Chu, and Tsai (2005), Nathan and Chen (2004), and Park and Shin (2004). Chang, Chu, and Tsai (2005) conclude that "Confucian values have a negative influence on democratic values." They believe that the democratic future in East Asia is bright, but only because modernization will undermine support for Confucian values. Nathan and Chen (2004) similarly find that "people with traditional values in all three societies (Taiwan, China, Hong Kong) were highly unlikely to hold democratic values" (see also Chu et al. 2008). Finally, Park and Shin (2004; see also see also Shin, Chey, and Kim 1989) are more equivocal in their study of Asian values in South Korea, finding that certain Confucian values undermine democratic values, others support it, and still others have no effect. Clearly, much more empirical work remains to be done on this important dispute.

Our work differs from most existing empirical studies in several respects. Nathan and Chen (2004) specifically address the question of Confucianism and democracy, but they base their findings on data only from 1993, before it was completely apparent that Taiwan would fully democratize. It was not until 1996, after all, that Taiwan held its first direct presidential election (Roy 2003:195-202). Our study compares data from 1995, in the midst of Taiwan's democratization, with those from 2001 and 2009, after Taiwan had fully democratized and the Democratic Progressive Party had gained control of the presidency (Roy 2003:227-240). The three data sets allow us to evaluate whether Confucianism has different effects in an emerging democracy as opposed to a more mature one.

Chang, Chu, and Tsai (2005) do look at the more recent 2001 data, but we see potential problems with the way in which they operationalize Confucianism. In particular, they conflate all "traditional Confucian ethics" into a single composite index. The six component indicators, however, seem to overemphasize the particular Confucian value that Park and Shin (2004) call "Group Primacy" (questions Q064, Q065, and CN74E) but underemphasize the Confucian value of Social Harmony (only question Q066). While their resulting index seems to hold together well, their use of a composite index could obscure the extent to which different components of Confucianism may have divergent effects on support for liberal democracy. This suspicion is at least partly confirmed by Park and Shin, who break Confucianism into its chief component values instead of creating a single composite index. Using Korean data, these authors find that the individual Confucian values, which they labeled Social Hierarchy, Social Harmony, Group Primacy, and Anti-Pluralism, all had statistically significant effects on opposition to authoritarianism, but those effects were signed in different directions. Such results suggest that using a composite Confucianism index or a related technique (e.g., factor analysis treating Confucianism as a single dimension) is not theoretically justifiable. Since Park and Shin look only at Korean data, it seemed useful to conduct a parallel study of Taiwan.

This analysis also sheds light on which of the two Weberian theories of ideology is most relevant to the Taiwanese experience with liberal democracy. Do the data confirm Weber's view that Confucianism is inherently conservative, as many theorists contend, or do the data suggest that the tradition is malleable, open to alternative interpretations, and potentially supportive of democracy?

Data and Models

In order to test these hypotheses, we analyzed three Taiwanese public opinion surveys. The first is the 1995 Taiwanese subset of the World Values Survey.[1] The Survey Research Center of Academia Sinica in Taipei fielded the N=780 poll in July of 1995 using face-to-face personal interviews in Mandarin, Taiwanese, and Hakka. The second poll is the Taiwanese subsample of the 2001 Asian Barometer Survey.[2] Again using face-to-face interviews, Academia Sinica sampled 1,416 Taiwanese voting-eligible citizens over age nineteen using the Probability Proportional to Size method during June-July of 2001. The third study, which we privately commissioned, was conducted by TNS Research International during September 2-13, 2009. The telephone-based poll used random-digit dialing to select households' numbers and then quota-sampled individual respondents within the households by region, gender, and age according to the 2007 Taiwan Census of Population. This procedure produced 1,000 usable respondents before weighting.

For the purposes of this chapter, we will define Confucianism as an ethical system that places primary emphasis on family loyalty, social hierarchies, and social harmony (Yao 2000; Oldstone-Moore 2003; Goldin 2011). We were able to identify usable questions from each of the surveys to measure these three aspects of Confucianism. Out of the universe of all questions in the 1995 and 2001 surveys, we chose one indicator for each of the three Confucian values. For the 1995 survey, our indicator of family loyalty was whether a main goal of the respondent's life has been "to make my parents proud." Our measure of support for social hierarchies was if the respondent agreed that people in Taiwan should have "greater respect for authority." Finally, the item for social harmony was whether interviewees believed that an employee should "follow one's superior's instructions at work even when one does not fully agree with them." In the 2001 survey, the indicator for family loyalty was whether "for the sake of the family, the individual should put his or her personal interests second." The measure for social hierarchies was whether, when there is a quarrel, "we should ask an elder to resolve the dispute." The question for social harmony asked whether the best way to resolve conflict with a neighbor was to "accommodate the other person." Our 2009 survey measured the three major Confucian values with questions on the extent to which the respondent puts "his or her family's wishes" [家人的願望] above his or her own, "follows the advice of elders" [管長輩的意見], and would "give in to a coworker" [接納我的同事] if the respondent "thought him or her in the wrong" [認爲他是錯的].

Our first dependent variable was support for democracy. In 1995, the four indicators we used to create a democracy index were: whether interviewees supported "having a strong leader who does not have to bother with parliament and elections" and "having a democratic political system" and whether they agreed with the statements "democracies are not good at maintaining order" and "democracy may have problems, but it is better than any other form of government." The 2001 indicators were: a one-to-ten scale measuring "to what extent would you want our country to be democratic now?"; whether "democracy is better than any other kind of government"; and whether "we should get rid of parliament and elections and have a strong leader decide things."

Freedom of speech was our second dependent variable. The one indicator for the 1995 survey was whether one of the country's chief aims should be "protecting freedom of speech." In 2001, the two freedom-of-speech questions were whether the government should "decide if certain ideas should be allowed to be discussed in society," and if "a political leader should tolerate the views of those who challenge his political ideals." For support for women's rights, we used the following three indicators from the 1995 survey: "when jobs are scarce, men should have more right to a job than women"; "on the whole men make better political leaders than women do"; and "a university education is more important for a boy than for a girl." The one women's rights indicator for the 2001 survey was "a man will lose face if he works under a female supervisor." In our 2009 survey, finally, the relevant item for indigenous rights was whether the government 1. "has already spent too much [已經花太多]," 2. "should spend more [應該花更多]," or 3. spends "just the right amount [恰到好]" of money and time on "aboriginal matters [原住民的事情]."

TABLE 3.1
Support for Confucian Values, 1995-2009

1995 World Values Survey	Percent Agree
Make Parents Proud (family loyalty)	63.4
Greater Respect for Authority (social hierarchies)	44.8
Follow Superior's Instructions at Work (social harmony)	15.4
2001 Asian Barometer	
Put Family First (family loyalty)	86.2
Elders Should Resolve Disputes (social hierarchies)	68.9
Give in to Avoid Conflict (social harmony)	46.1
2006 Asian Barometer	
Put Family First (family loyalty)	88.4
Do Not Question Authority of Teachers (social hierarchies)	29.2
Give in to Avoid Conflict (social harmony)	39.8
2009 TNS Study	
Follow Family's Wishes (family loyalty)	33.0
Follow Elders' Advice (social hierarchies)	19.0
Give in to Co-Worker (social harmony)	52.5

The first issue we explored was the extent to which Taiwan is a Confucian society. Table 3.1 indicates the percentage of our respondents who agreed with each of the indicators of the three different Confucian values in the four surveys. (This table also includes a second wave of the Asian Barometer, from 2006.) Because the question wording is not identical among these polls, over-time comparison must remain tentative at best. However, these results demonstrate that in both 1995 and 2001, respondents gave overwhelming support to at least one indicator of a Confucian value and majority or near-majority support to a second, but lower acquiescence to a third. In 1995, for example, nearly two thirds of interviewees agreed that one of the major life goals was to "make their parents proud," while in 2001 a slightly larger percentage affirmed that a person should put his or her interests "second" for the sake of the family. In the 2006 survey, respondents once again strongly supported family loyalty but seemed significantly less enthusiastic about social hierarchies and social harmony. In 2009, respondents gave majority support to our indicator of social harmony but tended to disagree with the Confucian values of family loyalty and, especially, social hierarchies. So while we still seem justified in treating Taiwan as a society based on Confucian values, the level of popular acquiescence in such a worldview might well be slipping as the island democratizes (see parallel discussion in chapter 1).

In order to test the net effect of Confucianism on liberal democracy, we used ordinary least-squares or Logit regression to estimate the effect of each of the three Confucian values on the various dependent variables for the 1995, 2001, and 2009 surveys. Although we focused mainly on the effect of the three Confucian values, we also controlled for such demographic variables as education, income, religious identification, gender, age, ethnicity, and urbanicity (see full regression results in Tables A3.1 and A3.2 of the Statistical Appendix).

Findings

Before we report the regression results, it would be useful to describe the levels of support for each of the liberal-democratic variables that we seek to explain. Overall, these descriptive data suggest that ordinary Taiwanese generally support liberal-democratic values. As early as 1995, for example, 83.5 percent of interviewees agreed that democracy was "better than any other form of government." In 2001, 71.6 percent opposed having the government decide "whether certain ideas should be discussed in society." More than three quarters of respondents (76.1 percent) in 1995 rejected the idea that a university education is more important for men than for women. For indigenous rights, meanwhile, 38 percent believed in 2009 that the government should "spend more money and time" on aborigines.

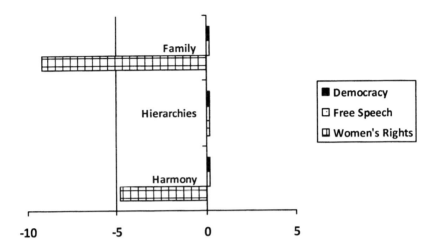

Figure 3.1. Confucian Values and Support for Liberal Democracy in 1995 (percent change).

Figure 3.1 presents the results of our regression analysis for 1995. No Confucian value had any statistically significant effect on either democratization or freedom of speech, either positively or negatively. As the corresponding bars pointing to the left show, however, family loyalty and social harmony did substantially undermine support for women's rights.

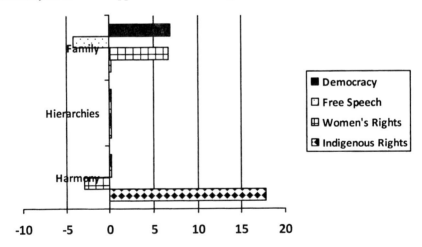

Figure 3.2. Confucian Values and Support for Liberal Democracy in 2001 and 2009 (percent change).

By 2001 (see figure 3.2), the relationship between Confucian and liberal-democratic values has partly changed. The indicator of social hierarchies still fails to achieve statistical significance for any of the liberal-democratic variables. Although social harmony continues to undermine women's rights slightly, family loyalty is now *boosting* support for gender equality. Moreover, this latter Confucian value is also positively correlated with belief in democracy. Finally, social harmony seems to increase respect for the rights of indigenous Taiwanese dramatically.[3] At the mass level, then, it seems that Confucianism is gradually transforming itself into an ideology that either has no impact on such political attitudes or bolsters enthusiasm for certain aspects of democracy and human rights.

Some of our control variables produced a few unanticipated results (see Tables A3.1 and A3.2 in the Statistical Appendix). Despite the widespread assumption that Taiwan is a society riven with ethnicity-based political strife (see Wang 2003), our three indicators of ethnicity (i.e., Mainlander, Yuanzhumin, and Other Ethnicity [largely Hakka]) produced almost nothing that reached statistical significance. In 2001, no ethnicity variable had any effect. In 1995, meanwhile, ethnicity only mattered for support for woman's rights. Not surprisingly, however, higher education led to increased support for democratization in both years. Also intriguing is the effect of being a woman. In 1995, women were, everything else being equal, *less likely* to support democratization (b = -.359, p < .05) and freedom of speech (b = -.462, p < .05). By 2001, however, being female had no effect on democratization and freedom of speech but did increase support for women's rights (b = .434, p < .05). In 1995, being a Christian seems to have increased enthusiasm for democratization (b = .835, p < .05). Perhaps because many leaders or supporters of the democracy movement were Christian clergy (Shih 1998:6-51; Rigger 1999:117-118; Roy 2003:169; Rubinstein 2006), Christian laity undoubtedly received pro-democracy cues from the pulpit or their co-religionists. Once democracy had become an established fact in 2001, however, the Christian variable no longer achieved statistical significance.

Conclusion

One important finding from our analysis is that Confucian norms do not consistently undermine liberal democracy in Taiwan. None of the three Confucian values (i.e., family loyalty, social hierarchies, and social harmony) reduces support for democratization. Only on women's rights do we find any possible pattern of conflict between human rights and Confucian values. Social harmony, in particular, seems always to decrease adherence to the rights of women. Family loyalty, on the other hand, showed a similar pattern in 1995 but by 2001 was *boosting* support for women's rights.

A second key result is that our empirical outcome appears to have bolstered our case for considering each Confucian value separately *à la* Park and Shin instead of conflating the various components of Confucianism into a single index. In 2001, for example, the effect of social harmony on women's rights is statistically significant and negative, the influence of family loyalty is statistically significant but positive, and the impact of social hierarchies does not achieve statistical significance. Had we combined these three elements into a single scale, we would have missed the real variations among their effects.

Our data do indicate that Confucian values remain strong in Taiwanese society. Overall levels of support for these key values seem to be declining, however. On the one hand, ordinary Taiwanese who adhere to Confucian values do not necessarily associate them with authoritarianism as the political elites we interviewed for chapter 2 almost uniformly do. Perhaps non-elites have a more nuanced understanding of the tradition than do their more politically committed counterparts. Yet paradoxically, mass-level decline in support for these values indicates that more Taiwanese are abandoning the tradition wholesale, as is largely true for pro-democratic political elites. In the next chapter, we investigate whether the way in which the government has transmitted Confucianism at different periods of Taiwan's political history might help to explain changes in the relationship between this ideology and citizens' adherence to liberal democracy.

Notes

1. "European and World Values Survey Integrated Data File, 1999-2002, Release I," Ronald Inglehart et al., University of Michigan, second ICPSR version, January 2005, ICPSR #3975. Neither the producers nor the distributors of these data are responsible for our analysis or interpretations.

2. Data analyzed in this chapter were collected by the East Asia Barometer Project (2000-2004), which was co-directed by Professors Hu Fu and Chu Yunhan and received major funding from Taiwan's Ministry of Education, Academia Sinica, and National Taiwan University. The Asian Barometer Project Office (www.asianbarometer.org) is responsible only for data distribution. The authors are grateful to the above directors and institutes for these data, but neither the producers nor distributors are responsible for our analysis or interpretations.

3. Not relevant for the four major theories, none of the control variables (i.e., income, gender, urbanicity, and marital status) reached statistical significance.

Chapter 4
The Treatment of Confucianism in Taiwanese Textbooks Before and After Democratization

The Master said, "The accomplished scholar is not a utensil."
Confucius (1971:150), Analects (II. xii)

In an effort to stem a rise in bullying, drug use, and gang problems in public schools, the Taiwanese Ministry of Education in February of 2011 proposed a new curriculum that would promote civic and moral values. The idea was to expose students to the four great Confucian classics: *Analects*, *The Doctrine of the Mean*, *The Great Learning*, and *The Mencius*. In response, students and teachers began a Facebook petition to pressure the government to modify its policy. Political leaders weighed in as well. An editorial from the pro-China *Commercial Times* insisted that the Confucian values of respect for others, social harmony, and hard work would benefit Taiwanese youth, while a commentary published in the pro-independence *Liberty Times* countered that ancient Chinese texts were pedagogically unhelpful for a modern democratic culture like Taiwan's. This latter editorial further asserted that "whether in blood or culture, we have many differences with Chinese people and culture. The leaders of the KMT and China's Communist Party have the same goal of suppressing democracy while advocating Chinese culture" (China Realtime Report 2011).

While it might seem surprising that such a seemingly innocuous proposal would become a source of such heated political controversy, this debate suggests that the Confucian tradition in Taiwan and much of East Asia is neither innocent nor uncontested. As is true for many or most political issues in Taiwan, this plan was inevitably read through the lens of cross-strait relations. Opponents interpreted the educational program as a heavy-handed effort by the KMT government to impose Chinese values on Taiwanese who are increasingly asserting their distinctive cultural and political identity. Supporters of the proposal countered that traditional Confucian values are as relevant and important as ever. That China had been recently engaged in an orchestrated campaign to revive interest in Confucius on the mainland and elsewhere through its state-sponsored

Confucius Institutes further fanned the flames of political mistrust. Despite the Master's admonition which opened this chapter that the "accomplished scholar," and presumably educators, are not simply "utensils" [器] or "tools" to be used and manipulated by others, that is precisely what has happened to the teaching of Confucianism in Taiwan and China.

This chapter focuses on how the Confucian tradition has been transmitted at different moments in Taiwan's history. As we have demonstrated in the preceding chapters, Confucianism may be interpreted in various ways, different values can be stressed, and alternative political systems can be legitimated by the Confucian corpus. Essentially no "neutral" Confucianism exists that is not shaped, at least in part, by those interpreting and passing on the tradition. To analyze this process of interpretation, we will look at how the Taiwanese educational curriculum covered Confucius and Confucianism during the pre- and post-authoritarian eras. Focusing on education is an ideal way to explore how Confucian values have been understood and transmitted. As an agent of political socialization, no institution is more crucial than the schools. The choice of topics and educational materials is a political decision that reflects social values and governmental priorities. Confucianism was, as we will show below, a core part of the educational curriculum in both authoritarian and democratic Taiwan. What differed in these distinct periods was how Confucianism was taught, which of its many values were highlighted, and what connection was drawn between the tradition and the world of politics.

Educational Setting

A curriculum is not created in a vacuum; it is instead a product of economic, political, and historical factors that profoundly shape how the material is taught in the schools. This link between politics and education is transparent in the case of Taiwan during the authoritarian rule of Chiang Kai-shek. The Nationalists' defeat at the hands of the Communist Party and their subsequent retreat to Taiwan posed a series of challenges to the KMT. Chief among them was to provide an explanation for their loss, prepare for a possible military attack from mainland China, offer a justification for KMT rule in Taiwan, and direct the island country's future direction. Educational policy became a key instrument in this process.

KMT educational policy was in many respects quite progressive. Article 159 of the 1946 Republic of China Constitution affirmed that "all citizens have an equal opportunity to an education," while article 160 mandated universal schooling for all children "from six to twelve of years of age" and guaranteed that "poor families shall be supplied with books by the government" (Government Information Office 2009: Appendix III). In 1968, state-funded compulsory education was expanded from six to nine years. These were ambitious goals compared to what the Nationalists had accomplished when they governed mainland China, and the KMT was eager to demonstrate that their educational system was superior to that of the Communists. During the years of authoritarian rule in

Taiwan, the number of schools and students more than doubled, while the illiteracy rate fell from 24 to 9 percent (Pai 1995:38-40).

As much as the Nationalists promoted literacy and technical expertise, article 162 of the Constitution also affirmed that all public and private education would be "subject to state supervision." Through the newly created Ministry of Education and its affiliated "Taiwan Provisional Department of Education," the national government controlled all areas associated with curriculum, personnel, financing, and the crucial area of textbook editing. Moreover, article 158 made clear that the goal of education was to "develop" the "national spirit" in citizens (Government Information Office 2009: Appendix III). What this phrase came to mean was that education promoted Chinese nationalism, rationalized KMT rule on the island, and indoctrinated students with the message that Taiwan's sacred mission was the recovery of mainland China (Tsai 2002). In her review of civics curriculum during the authoritarian period, Liu Meihui (2006:74) similarly concludes that the overall purpose of such material was to "develop good citizens who upheld the law, showed obedience to authority, and were willing to serve the community and country."

The KMT also linked its educational mission to that of the party's founder, Sun Yat-sen, and his Three Principles of the People: nationalism, democracy, and the welfare of the people. A 1980 official publication of the Education Ministry (Department of Education 1980:2-3) defined the purpose of nationalism as "welding the people together through a feeling of national identity" and arousing "a patriotic enthusiasm that spurs deep patriotic actions." More than just lip service was paid to democracy; being "democratic" was one way distinguish Taiwan from Communist China, and it served as the political goal toward which the country was moving in principle (and also, at least in the long run, in reality). However, this long-term democratic ideal supposedly had to be delayed because of the emergency situation in which the state found itself. An official party theorist, writing about Chiang Kai-shek's understanding of Sun's principle of democracy, claimed that "President Chiang Kai-shek has most cogently remarked that the spirit of democracy is manifested in discipline whose concrete significance is manifested in the rule of law" (Wang 1981:185). Similarly, the Department of Education (1980:2-3) of the era also partially defined democracy as "cultivat[ing] respect for the laws and orderly habits."

The Confucian tradition became an ideological ally in this larger endeavor. A speech delivered by Chiang (1968) to the nation's educational corps demonstrates how the Nationalists understood Confucius and the relevance of his message for education. The speech was given on September 28, which is celebrated in Taiwan as Confucius' birthday, or "Teacher's Day." 1968 marked the height of the Cultural Revolution in mainland China, where Mao and the Red Guards attacked Confucius for his supposed "feudalism" and "anti-revolutionary" teachings. In his speech, Chiang thus noted that "today the mainland Chinese Communist bandits are in the process of insanely destroying Chinese culture, and they view Confucianism as an enemy." Chiang countered that "it is a mistake to view [Confucius] as backward or feudal. . . . We should instead esteem Confucius as great and sincerely believe in the eternally valid nature of Confucianism." And what is the core of that message that Chiang hoped the country's teachers might appreciate? The president summed it up this way:

> Confucius' educational thinking was based on wisdom, benevolent empathy [仁] and courage. . . . The purpose of education is to produce a person who behaves correctly, a dignified and proper Chinese person. . . . The result of proper etiquette is for each member of the family or society to value his or her proper role and to follow strict discipline.

In short, Chiang valued Confucianism and wanted it to be a part of the system of education, but it was a traditional, conservative form of the tradition that he wanted articulated. In Confucius, Chiang found a thinker whom he believed taught respect for authority and unquestioned loyalty to the dictates of government. They were precisely the values that the minority, KMT mainlanders, would need to justify their authoritarian rule over the majority, native Taiwanese. Equally significant, however, was that Confucius was the pre-eminent Chinese thinker of all time and could become a core part of the KMT policy to Sinicize the Taiwanese population on the island. For the KMT, there was no better way to demonstrate the perceived superiority of Chinese culture and values, and by implication to downplay Taiwanese traditions, than to introduce students to Confucius. The same thinking led educational authorities to require extensive consideration of the political thought of Sun Yat-sen, the founder of the KMT, and to teach all classes in Mandarin, rather than Taiwanese. In all of these measures, the party dictated educational policy from the very top. Nationally standardized textbooks were required in all classes until 1996, those textbooks were closely edited by the Ministry of Education, and the content was designed to advance the nationalist interests of the KMT (Su 2006). During the martial-law era, the typical student was exposed to Confucianism in three academic subjects: social studies, history, and Chinese language. As one of our interviewees, Tsai Chi-hsun (2008), Secretary General of the Taiwan Association for Human Rights, ironically noted, "Anyone over the age of thirty in Taiwan was educated under a system that emphasized the importance of Confucianism in Chinese culture. The KMT took Confucius *very* seriously."

Education in democratic Taiwan is in many respects fundamentally different than it was during the authoritarian era. Notably, the entire educational system is much more professionalized and less dictated by the national government. As an example, political control over textbooks has been loosened considerably. School administrators and teachers are now able to decide which of any number of textbooks will be used in the class. The content of the curriculum is also much changed. The values that are now highlighted in civics and social studies classes are more democratic and arguably less nationalistic than they once were (Liu 2011:79). Much more consideration is also given to such western-influenced ideas as gender rights, multiculturalism, and human rights. Su Ya-Chen (2006) notes that this transition in educational policy moved in concert with the country's gradual democratization.

What has not changed much in the pre- and post-authoritarian Taiwan is how much exposure the typical student gets to Confucius and Confucianism. In the martial-law era the curriculum included several hours per week of topics that would have included Confucius. In democratic Taiwan, Confucius is also included in at least three of the seven designated areas of learning: Chinese language and literature, social studies, and history. Together, these subjects constitute about half of the curriculum. Thus, Confucius was and is a significant part of the school day in the two time periods; what remains to be seen is how Confucius is explained and examined during the different eras.

To examine more concretely how Taiwanese textbooks covered Confucianism during the authoritarian and democratic periods, we first selected these three major subjects where this ideology would be most likely to be taught (i.e., social studies, Chinese language or literature, and history). The first author then obtained copies of representative texts, all roughly at the same grade level, from the archives of the Textbook Resource Center [教科書資料中心] at the National Institute for Compilation and Translation [國立編譯館] (NICT) in Taipei or, in one case, from a North American research library. For each subject, at least one textbook was accessed from before the lifting of martial law in 1987, and another volume came from after democratization. In the end, we were able to locate three sixth-grade social studies textbooks (years 1968, 1968, and 2000), two elementary-level works on the Chinese language (years 1965 and 2001), and two late-elementary or early-middle-school history volumes (years 1960 and 2002). We then focused on the parts of each text that specifically discussed Confucius and/or Confucianism.

Confucius and Confucianism in the Past and Present

For our purposes, we wish to analyze three main themes when comparing the treatment of Confucius and Confucianism in the pre- and post-authoritarian eras. First, we will focus on how the textbooks describe Confucius, his role in Chinese history, and his place in contemporary Taiwanese society. Second, we will consider which of the many Confucian values are promoted in the different eras. Finally, we will evaluate how the particular Confucian values that are highlighted are interpreted in the two time periods.

In keeping with the KMT's interest in promoting Chinese culture and values in Taiwan and in defending the party's rule on the island, the textbooks from the martial-law period present Confucius as the epitome of Chinese superiority. A 1968 Social Studies text, for example, notes that "traditional Chinese culture is so splendid because it is based on Confucian doctrine and its five thousand years of history. . . . Five thousand years of Chinese history form such a splendid cultural tradition" (NICT 1968b:77-79). Teaching the centrality of Confucius to Chinese culture seems to have been effective. A martial-law era assessment by the Education Ministry (1973:266) noted that 91.8 percent of the student respondents at the end of the school year correctly identified Confucius as being "at the center of our country's traditional culture," which was an improvement of more than 10 percent from the beginning of the year.

One mark of the Master's importance is the influence that his thinking had on other cultures. In a section entitled "Chinese Culture Spreads to the West" a social studies book notes that "well-known scholars from the time in France, Germany, and other European countries studied the doctrines of Confucius, which they greatly admired" (NICT 1968a:6). Even more significantly, the books present Confucius as part of an almost holy trinity which includes Sun Yat-sen and Chiang Kai-shek (NICT 1968b:81):

> Dr. Sun (the founder of our nation) inherited traditional Chinese culture and developed it to create the profound Three Principles of the People. The President [Chiang Kai-shek] has presented the relationship between traditional culture and the Three Principles of the People in detail. . . . The implementation of the Three Principles of the People is a way to promote traditional Chinese culture.

The intent of such passages is to present the current political leadership in an unbroken line to the greatness of China's past. The book's treatment of Confucius' early life contains an almost hagiographic element. After noting where and when he was born, along with the fact that Confucius' father died when the boy was three, a 1960 history book comments that in his teenage years, Confucius "studied very hard, often forgetting to eat during the day and to sleep at night. . . . Despite his low position, he was very diligent and never neglected his duties. He therefore achieved great results" (NICT 1960:24-25). It is hard to avoid the conclusion that the readers were supposed to take from this message that they too should be diligent in their duties despite the hardships that they might face. In 1960, when this text was written, many Taiwanese faced the existential threat of a military invasion from Communist China.

The link between Confucius and Chinese culture is not lost in the post-authoritarian era, but the association between the past and the present is much more muted in the more recent texts. In describing his ongoing influence, a 2001 Chinese language and literature book (NICT 2001:56) notes that "two thousand five hundred years ago, there was a great educator who was born in China, Confucius. His theories greatly influenced Chinese culture. His educational ideas were especially influential and represented the most successful model for education." A 2000 social studies text (NICT 2000:78) explicates what was particularly unique, and presumably influential, about Confucius: "before Confucius, only the aristocracy had the opportunity to be educated. . . . He was the first person to teach commoners." Finally, the same text notes the universal ethical teaching of Confucius when it writes: "He also said: 'Do not do to other people things that you would not want done to yourself'" (2000:79). Thus, Confucius remains an historically significant figure in the recent books, but the universal values he promoted (education and the Golden Rule) are much more democratically inspired.

What is noticeably absent in the contemporary books is any attempt to connect Confucius to either Sun Yat-sen or Chiang Kai-shek, both of whom have dropped out entirely in the sections dealing with Confucius. Also, the book's consideration of Confucius' life takes on less of a devotional character; instead, the texts offer a much more straightforward biography (see Slingerland 2008). As might be expected, the basic outlines of that life history are essentially the same. The recent books note that Confucius' father died when the boy was only three years old and that Confucius and his mother were very poor. But, there is no discussion of Confucius' diligence or of his foregoing food and drink to study. Instead, a 2000 social studies text simply notes that "[a]s a child, Confucius learned to do various things, which widely expanded his experience and knowledge" (NICT 2000:77). Finally, the post-authoritarian books use a historical-critical method which places Confucius within his cultural context: "during the Spring and Autumn Period, the most famous systems of thought were Confucianism, Mohism, Taoism, and Legalism" (NICT 2002:42). In short, Confucianism was one of many belief systems that were and are historically important in China.

In their biographical account of Confucius' life, books in both the martial-law and democratic periods note that Confucius was himself involved in politics. But the texts give a different interpretation of that political leadership. A 1960 history book (NICT 1960:25-26) comments that "when Confucius was in his fifties, he became prime minister of the country of Lu." The book goes on to note that under his leadership, everything was "under control" in Lu, but that he resigned his position because of "powerful rival officials." The result, the book tells us, was "social turmoil[:] people became hard-hearted and killed each other." As a result, Confucius becomes indignant and levies this judgment on the politics of his day:

> "I want future generations to understand the situation nowadays. If an oral reprimand is not enough punishment, I will try to discipline them with my pen." He recorded all the major events of each country one by one and wrote a book called *Spring and Autumn Annals*. . . Afterwards, Mencius praised this book, saying: "Confucius wrote the *Spring and Autumn Annals*, which scared evil rulers and wicked people."

In what is a common theme in the martial-law books, the life of Confucius becomes symbolic of the Taiwanese experience, or at least representative of how the KMT understood the situation in Taiwan. In this case, Confucius' effective leadership (supposedly like that of Chiang Kai-shek) is undermined by powerful rival officials (Mao and the Communists). The result is social turmoil (the civil war between the Nationalists and the Communists). Defeated and disgusted, Confucius leaves the world of politics but writes about his indignation at the practices of his day for future generations to learn from. A more recent social studies book (NICT 2000:77-78) tells a somewhat similar tale of Confucius' life. Like the martial-law text, this work notes Confucius' political leadership. But, it provides little narrative for why he left politics and offers a different account of what he taught political leaders in subsequent years:

> Confucius traveled around different countries for fourteen years, explaining to political leaders his ideas about how to govern a country. His dream was to use the system of etiquette and ritual music to save this disorderedly society, but

not many people accepted his views. . . . He recorded all major events of each country, and wrote a book called the *Spring and Autumn Annals*. . . . He finally returned to Lu. After that, Confucius concentrated on education and writing.

While it is not as explicit in making a connection between the past and the present, in its own way the more recent textbook advances a particular understanding about politics from the life of Confucius. In this case, Confucius concentrates on education and writing to save his troubled society.

The textbooks from the two eras also differ in which Confucian values they highlight and/or in how they choose to interpret those values. It would be impossible to discuss Confucian ethics without saying that ren [仁] is, as a 1960s social studies text notes, "the starting point" for Confucianism (NICT 1968b:79). The book's discussion of ren opens by noting that the concept means benevolence, empathy, and helping others, all of which is relatively straightforward and noncontentious. However, in a lengthy paragraph the text links ren to social and political values that were central to the KMT (NICT 1968b:80-81):

> We can say more specifically: the driving force behind benevolence is honesty so that the Chinese treat each other with leniency, peacefulness, and impartiality, focusing on people's relations with one another, and stressing moderation, with the spirit of democracy. They should be able to do research and invent things and serve others, to help the needy and the foreigner as well. However, if there is a crucial moment for the nation, everyone will unite together and cooperate with each other. The essence of the highest form of ren is bravery in saving one's country, which is a concrete manifestation of benevolence. This ultimate form of ren is also the root of traditional Chinese culture.

The transition of the idea of ren in this single paragraph is illuminating. At the opening, ren is defined simply as benevolence. The next several sentences, however, implicitly link the idea of benevolence to what was the official KMT policy of the day, implementation of Sun Yat-sen's Three Principles of the People: nationalism, democracy, and the welfare of the people. As if the connection between nationalism and ren were not clearly enough drawn, the paragraph ends by asserting that the "highest form" of benevolence and the "root of traditional Chinese culture" is "bravery in serving one's country."

The post-martial law texts similarly note that ren is the "main idea" of Confucianism. The meaning of that value, however, differs from its earlier understanding. A later social studies text (NICT 2000:78-79) reads as follows:

> Confucius paid special attention to the policy of benevolent virtue, which is to love others. The implementation of the principle of benevolence is loyalty and forbearance. Loyalty means that everyone should perform his or her responsibility. Forbearance means showing consideration for others.

Whereas in the martial-law narratives, ren became a social and political virtue, in the democratic era, ren is primarily described in such privatized terms as benevolence, doing unto others as you would want done to you, mutual respect, and true compassion. When the contemporary texts explicitly link ren to politics, moreover, the result is very different from that during the martial-law era. A 2002 history text (NICT 2002:41) notes:

> Confucius advocated benevolence extending up the political level: political leaders should protect the people, love the people, and educate them with moral enlightenment. Confucius was also the first educator to advocate teaching everyone regardless of status, from the aristocracy to ordinary people. Because of his doctrine that there should be no discrimination in education, a view that is widely respected by the world, he is honored as a sage and teacher.

Even when ren is the basis for politics, in short, it promotes the rights of "ordinary" people and the very democratic notion of no discrimination in education.

Because vast numbers of stories and sayings are attributed to Confucius in the *Analects, The Great Learning, The Doctrine of the Mean*, and other ancient works in the Confucian tradition, one way to examine the values that undergird Taiwanese textbooks is to consider which of those stories they choose to relate. In a section entitled "the courtesy of Confucius," a martial-law-period Chinese language and literature book (NICT 1965:73-74) presents what might be considered an obscure passage:

> Confucius was always very polite to others. When he met an acquaintance on the road, he would always greet the person. If he came across a group of people, he would also get out of his vehicle. Once, the Chu defeated the country of Chen, occupied the Chen people's city, and required them to repair the fortifications. Confucius was sitting in his vehicle as he passed by this city in the country of Chen. Although he saw many people repairing the city wall, he did not get out of his vehicle to greet them. When his students found out, they were puzzled and asked him: "Why didn't you get out of your vehicle today when you saw so many people at the city?" Confucius said with a sigh: "If a country suffers from enemy aggression, people should work together to resist the foe. If the country is conquered, people should not work for the enemy. If people are not defending their country by fighting their opponents but instead are working for the enemy, what virtue is there in that?"

Under normal circumstances, the passage suggests, the polite and Confucian thing to do is to greet people and treat them with respect. However, the story related was not a "normal" situation. Instead, it tells of a time when the country of Chen had been overrun by its enemy, the Chu, who demanded that the vanquished Chen people repair the walls of the destroyed cities. Passing such a scene, Confucius refuses to get out of his vehicle and greet the people because to do so might imply support for the enemy and acquiescence in the current political state of affairs. It would have hardly been much of a stretch for Taiwanese pupils to understand this story as symbolic of their own situation vis-à-vis Communist China. Those living in Taiwan were like the Chen people who had been overrun by the Chu, or Communists. In such a situation, pure benevolence was not the order of the day, but rather resistance to the enemy and defense of the country constituted the height of virtuous behavior. The passage, in short, equates Confucian virtues with struggle against the Communist enemy.

Not only do the themes of this particular story appear to reinforce KMT doctrine, but the original source of this tale is not one of the authoritative "Four Books" or even one of the "Five Classics" of Confucianism. Instead, the account comes from scroll 4 [立節], paragraph 2, of the *Garden of Stories*, or *Shuo Yuan* [說苑] (Liu 2012), which was compiled by a Chinese librarian who was born four centuries after Confucius died (Nienhauser 1986:583-584).[1] Selecting such a non-canonical text indicates how desperate the KMT editors were to show that Confucius would have supported their policies. Yet the at least semi-fictional *Shuo Yuan* bear the same relationship to the much more authoritative *Analects* that, say, the children's cartoon *VeggieTales* does to the Dead Sea Scrolls.

In contrast to its martial-law counterpart, a 2001 Chinese language and literature text (NICT 2001:56-58) highlights very different stories about Confucius. In one of these, Confucius critiques two of his students, Zi Gong [子貢] and Zi Lu [子路], because, despite their worldly success, they seemed to have left behind "their good values." Moreover, instead of the questionable source of the tale in the 1965 text, the standard *Analects* (I.xv) provides most of the following sample:

> Zi Gong was the richest of all his students because he had the gift of running a business. Once, Zi Gong asked Confucius: "What do you think about a rich person who is not proud of himself and a poor person who does not bribe others?" As soon as he asked this question, Confucius knew that Zi Gong was proud of himself, and he said: "These kind of people, of course, are good. But it would be better that those who were joyful when they were poor still obeyed the system of etiquette now that they are rich."

While the worldly successful Zi Gong is humbled, the same 2001 text describes the "very poor" Yan Hui [顏回] as Confucius' "favorite" student:

> Yan Hui was from a very poor family background, lived in a dilapidated house, and led a very simple life. But he was very happy and studied hard. He was a very self-controlled, even-tempered person and never made the same mistake twice. No one could compare with him. Confucius profusely praised his habit of treating others well and studying hard. Confucius not only treated all of his students with respect, even though each one was so different, but he also paid attention to each individual's particular personality and gave the student customized instructions. This is why Confucius was so great: he taught all kinds of students according to their various abilities.

The Confucius in the contemporary text, in short, promotes the very liberal ideas of treating every person with equal respect, paying attention to each person's individual personality, and teaching people according to their various abilities regardless of class background ("no discrimination in education"; see also NICT 2002:41). Of course, even contemporary editors must make some interpretive choices when selecting such passages, but in their defense, the compilers of 2001 relied on accounts from the authoritative *Analects* (VI.ii; XI.vi; XV.xxxviii) instead of a collection of Chinese fairy tales.

Conclusion

Perhaps one way to make sense of these findings given the results from the previous two chapters is to hypothesize that most of the older, pro-democracy political elites that we interviewed for chapter 2 were exposed to a form of official Confucianism in the schools that was little more than KMT propaganda. Thus, they naturally rejected Confucian values as inherently undemocratic. Our typical mass-level respondent from chapter 3, in contrast, likely had a different experience with Confucianism. Some percentage of the interviewees would have been taught the more democracy-friendly version of Confucianism that began to arise after the lifting of martial law, which might explain why any connections between support for Confucian values and opposition to liberal democracy are weak at best in the previous chapter.

The different uses of Confucianism in the pre and post-martial law textbooks also highlight the larger point that educational systems are greatly affected by the political context in which they are formed. This influence is relatively easy to identify in the martial-law era, when educational officials actively sought to forge a sense of identity with the Republic of China virtually out of whole cloth. This national consciousness was a hybrid of place (Taiwan and mainland China), ideology (Three Principles of the People), and values (Chinese identity). As we noted above, a reconfigured Confucianism played its part in promoting Chinese consciousness and in advancing a set of personal, social, and political values beneficial to the KMT. The nexus between Confucianism and the needs of the nation state are not nearly as transparent in the more recent textbooks. The rise of a politically insulated and professional educational class insures greater fidelity on their part to a "neutral" incorporation of Confucianism into the curriculum. Still, one has to wonder if there is not some "proof-texting" being employed by officials who now instead want to expose students to a more democracy-friendly Confucius.

Note

1. When we initially read this passage from the textbook, we were unable to locate it in any of the canonical Confucian works. We therefore contacted a number of scholars of ancient Chinese thought for advice. Ultimately, we learned that the incident was indeed not from one of the "Four Books" or "Five Classics" but was instead taken from the *Shuo Yuan*, which Professor Edward Slingerland (2011) describes as full of "all sorts of apocryphal Confucius stories." We are very grateful to Prof. Slingerland and to Professor Paul R. Goldin (2011), who identified the original source of the story.

Chapter 5
The Role of Confucianism in Taiwanese Legislative Debates over Democratization and Human Rights

With the right men the growth of government is rapid, just as vegetation is rapid in the earth; and moreover, their government might be called an easily growing rush. Therefore, the administration of government lies in getting proper men.

Confucius (1971:405), *The Doctrine of the Mean* (xx)

Confucian principles no longer work in practice. Witness the fact that for thousands of years no one has really succeeded in ruling an empire with Confucian principles of government.

Japanese journalist and educator Fukuzawa (2008:72) Yukichi,
An Outline of a Theory of Civilization

Politically, the pan-green *Taipei Times* and pan-blue *China Post* agree on almost nothing. An editorial in the *Taipei Times* (2012), for example, interpreted the 2012 presidential election won by the KMT incumbent Ma Ying-jeou as a "loss of national sovereignty" to mainland China, whom it not-so-subtly accused of manipulating the election so that the PRC could eventually "collect on the political debt that Ma has racked up" to the Communists. On the same day, *The China Post* (2012a) countered that the election proved that "an honest Ma has proved incorruptible and the voters turned out in droves to keep the man of probity at the helm of the state." In short, the pan-Blue and pan-Green rarely interpret political events in the same way.

Nonetheless, on one issue the otherwise deeply divided parties agree: the Taiwanese Legislative Yuan is an utter embarrassment. A 2011 article in *Foreign Policy* named the Yuan as one of the five least competent parliaments in the world, taking its place alongside the likes of Belgium, Japan, Iraq, and Afghanistan in a legislative hall of shame (Abadi 2011). The report cited the widespread political corruption of its members, hyper-partisan politics, legislative gridlock as the political norm, and the fact that fighting—even physically— between blue and green legislators is more common than is their cooperating on public policy. In response to the *Foreign Policy* analysis, the same papers that had such opposing views of the presidential election used almost identical language in editorials slamming the Legislative Yuan. The Chinese version of the *Taipei Times* (Low 2012) decried the Yuan for its failure to "safeguard taxpayer funds" and for the "vote-buying convictions" of five of its members, and the paper demanded that members of the Yuan "fulfill their duties as the people's gatekeepers." Not to be outdone, the *China Post* (2012b) opined that the hallmark of the Yuan was its "brawling and histrionics." It hoped that the new legislature would include fewer "selfish, incompetent morons." If nothing else, the Legislative Yuan should take some pride in having brought the blue and green press to an identical position.

It is difficult to imagine a legislative body with a history as unique as that of Taiwan's Legislative Yuan. It was formally established in 1928 by Chiang Kai-shek and was based on Sun Yat-sen's Three Principles of the People and Five-Power Constitution. Sun's political views were bifurcated. While he promoted the goals of democracy and emphasized the need for a separation of powers, he also argued that China was not ready for full democracy and required a period of political tutelage to prepare them for that system. During the period of "political tutelage," which lasted from 1928 until ratification of the Republic of China Constitution in 1946, members of the Legislative Yuan were selected by the President, effectively under his control and that of the KMT, and the body did not act as a democratic check on executive power. The ROC Constitution expanded the role of the Legislative Yuan, making it the "highest legislative organ of the state" with significant powers. Elections were held in 1948 to select its 760 members, but before constitutional government could be established in China, the Nationalists lost the war against the Communists, and the government was forced to move to Taiwan. Roughly half of the elected members of the Legislative Yuan came to Taiwan during the civil-war period (Bellows 2003:4-7).

The relocation of the National Government to Taiwan made it impossible to hold another election as seats in the Legislative Yuan were based upon district lines in mainland China. Consequently, those legislators elected in 1948 who made the exodus to Taiwan served for over forty years without ever standing for reelection, a situation that came to be described as the "Non-reelection Congress." Moreover, before leaving mainland China, the National Assembly drafted the "Temporary Provisions Effective during the Period of National Mobilization for the Suppression of the Communist Rebellion [動員戡亂時期臨時條款]." This legislation gave the President the right to establish martial law, which was put into place beginning in 1949 in Taiwan. Not only was the membership of the Legislative Yuan frozen during this period, but the body had little to no independent political power. Several supplementary elections were held between 1969 and 1989 to replace members who retired or died off and to fill newly created legislative seats in districts within Taiwan, but under martial law the government restricted competition for those seats to members of the KMT. Liberalization intensified toward the end of Chiang Ching-kuo's presidency (Taylor 2000). The democratization of Taiwan reached the Legislative Yuan when multi-party elections were held for the first time in 1992 with no seats held over from the Non-reelection Congress (Nathan 1993). Since that election, the

Legislative Yuan has gradually assumed its constitutional role as the chief legislative body with the power to pass laws and review the budget.[1]

The purpose of this chapter is to examine the nexus between Confucian ideology and key laws passed as Taiwan was democratizing. Specifically, we want to focus on the ideological rationale for the democratically inspired legislation, and to probe what role, if any, Confucianism assumed in the arguments presented. The legislative debates that we describe below occurred at different moments in the Legislative Yuan's history. The Civic Organizations Act of 1989 entered the law books prior to full democratization and the election of a representative legislative body, while the other three bills received approval after the Legislative Yuan became a popularly elected branch of government.

Civic Organizations Act, 1989

The restrictions on association goes back at least as far as a 1908 Qing dynasty law that severely curtailed the rights of civic and political groups. In 1914, Yuan Shih-kai's nominally Republican government issued the Public Security Police Force Ordinance [治安警察條例], maintaining such restrictions on civil society even after the end of dynastic China. During WWII, the Nationalists similarly passed the "Law on the Formation of People's Civic Organizations during the Period of Emergency Mobilization [非常時期人民團體組織法]" in 1942, which disallowed the political opposition (Shih 2012). When they fled to Taiwan in 1949, the KMT thus brought this law with them. Before 1989, political parties other than the KMT were officially illegal. While the Tangwai [黨外], or literally "outside the party," movement had been mobilizing and even running candidates for public office for more than a decade, no other party could receive explicit government approval (Tien 1989:95-103; Chang and Chiu 2005:II:82-83). The intent of the new Civic Organizations Act [人民團體法], therefore, was to open up the electoral system to genuine multi-party competition (Rigger 1999:114-124).

Debate on this bill was unusual for several reasons. Martial law had only been lifted in 1987. The Legislative Yuan had not itself been reformed into a fully democratic, multi-party body. And while some non-KMT representatives took part in the proceedings, the chamber as a whole was dominated by the Nationalists. The final outcome of the bill was never in doubt because the KMT government under Lee Teng-hui had itself proposed the measure. However, in a letter that the Ministry of the Interior sent to the legislature, one sees a hint of an incipient Confucianism in support of the measure (*Legislative Yuan Official Gazette* [立法院公報]1988:185):

> It has been more than forty-five years since this State of Emergency Civic Organizations Act was announced in 1942. . . . Because of the significant changes in our social structure and the flourishing growth of all kinds of organizations, it has been hard to adapt this law to the current needs of the community. Although our county is still in a time of mobilization, we should

continue unceasingly to promote constitutional democracy. Therefore, adding the regulation of political groups will help get the professional groups, social groups (organizations) and political groups to follow the Constitution and legal process, to participate in various activities, and to serve the national community.

This language suggests that while the government was promoting democracy, the authorities believed that the newly formed groups would primarily be concerned with the national rather than parochial interest. Arguably, this rationale harkens back to a conservative Confucianism that prioritizes an orderly, stable society.

On the other hand, when the Interior Ministry provides a justification for specific parts of the bill, it does so by referring to classic democratic values. For example, the Ministry defends the termination of the "state of emergency" [非常時期] and "period of mobilization" [動員勘亂時期] by claiming to want to "establish the normal rule of law." At other points in the debate, the KMT asserts the need to "establish a democratic process," "protect the equal competition of all political parties," and "ensure [governmental] neutrality" (*Legislative Yuan Official Gazette* 1988:44-45).

For their part, the few Tangwai members in the Legislative Yuan implicitly challenged the notion that creating a full-throttled democracy was consistent with some Confucian notion of stability, order, and decorum. Even in a debate that for understandable reasons was very mild, Tangwai representative You Ching [尤清] chastised his KMT counterparts for their initial failure to negotiate the terms of the bill with the opposition (*Legislative Yuan Official Gazette* 1988:43):

> The main reason why DPP members were subjected to a comprehensive exclusion when the committee reviewed the draft amendment of this law was because the DPP Legislative Yuan members were proposing to delete all of chapter 9. . . . therefore, [my] DPP colleagues were left out of the review.

Moreover, Tangwai delegate Chiu Lien-hui [邱連輝] takes this argument a step further in his very specific critique of the KMT: "The KMT, with its four decades of political baggage, was afraid that the opposition party would target the KMT and undermine its political reform during an electoral campaign" (*Legislative Yuan Official Gazette* 1988:45). Ironically, future-DPP members You and Chiu anticipate what would come to Taiwanese politics in general and the Legislative Yuan in particular: deep ethnic divisions, hyper-partisanship, and periodic physical assaults on the floor of the legislature (*Daily Mail* 2007). While President Lee might have imagined a fusion of democratization and conservative Confucianism, the subsequent reality has been far different.

Repeal of the Publishing Act, 1999

Even before the KMT government relocated to Taiwan in 1949, the party had moved to restrict press freedom as early as 1930. In that year, the Nationalist Legislative Yuan passed the "Publishing Act," which became the basis for legal restriction on publications for nearly seven decades. Over the years, the government revised the statute six times to reflect changing political realities, but these alterations did not fundamentally loosen control over the media. In combination with the establishment of martial law in Taiwan, the "Publishing Act" had a very chilling effect on journalists' willingness and ability to investigate political malfeasance, express their opposition to official policies, and publish their writing (Council for Cultural Affairs 2011). As the democratization movement gained steam in the late 1970s and the regime appeared to give independent media some room to maneuver, the pro-democracy magazines *Formosa* and *The Eighties* began publication (Rigger 1999:116-118). This relative freedom proved ephemeral, however, when the government cracked down on such publications and arrested a number of journalists. In one notorious incident, the authorities pressured *Freedom Era* editor Cheng Nan-jung so much in 1989 that he committed suicide (Li 2002:142-144; Roy 2003:175-176). The lifting of martial law nonetheless created an opening for activists to press for greater media freedom, but it was not until a decade later that the notorious Publishing Act was repealed.

Having originated in the KMT-led Executive Yuan, the proposal to abolition the Publishing Act was assured of ultimately passing. During the debate on the bill, no one argued to retain the Act as it was. Those who did question aspects of the repeal legislation raised potential concerns about the possible effects of media monopolies. Pan-blue member Yao Li-ming [姚立明], for example, commented (*Legislative Yuan Official Gazette* 1998:75-76):

> Originally, the media were the victim of the Publishing Act, but now the media will become a major threat to people's freedom. . . . How are the owners of media going to restrict their own internal direction of news coverage? More specifically, the management and operations of editors and news reporters will become an important issue in the future media environment. . . . There will be a future problem with freedom of the media within its own ranks, meaning that the owner of the media may limit the freedom of press of its workers.

Yao's views have nothing to do with a need for the government to restrict the press but instead focus on the potential danger of media consortia that may themselves limit the diversity of expressed opinion and interfere with reporters' ability to write what they wish. DPP legislator Roger Hsieh Tsung-min [謝聰敏], expressed a related concern that, with or without the Publishing Act, the government would continue to use its regulatory power to aid pro-KMT media outlets (*Legislative Yuan Official Gazette* 1998:78): "Doesn't it seem that you've benefitted those media organizations that belong to the ruling party?" Hsieh was speaking with some authority since he collaborated with Peng Ming-min during the 1960s, was arrested by Garrison Command [警備總司令部] secret police, was tortured, and was imprisoned multiple times (Peng 1972:124-127; Thornberry 2011). In response to Hsieh's query, the Director General of the official Government Information Office (GIO), Chen Chien-jen [程建人], suggested that, even if the KMT authorities had done so in the past, "We will definitely not do that" in the future (*Legislative Yuan Official Gazette* 1998:78).

On the other hand, supporters of a repeal of the Act consistently defended their views in liberal terms. For example, Cheng Nan-jung's widow and DPP Representative Yeh Chu-lan [葉菊蘭] powerfully connected the Publishing Act to the abuses of state power during the White Terror period (*Legislative Yuan Official Gazette* 1999a:42-43)

> Today, we understood that this press law is an evil law. I am pleased that the administrative branch can understand where the tide of public opinion is moving and that freedom of speech is the most important cornerstone of democracy. This Publishing Act not only curbs freedom of speech and hinders freedom of expression, but it also uses state resources to reward the activities of an authoritarian country and amplifies the voice of those already in power. After the repeal of this draconian law, there will be greater room for everyone to speak. Unrestricted journalism, freedom of speech, and an autonomous press will create more space for democracy and make civil society more robust.

In a similar way DPP legislator Tsai Ming-hsien [蔡明憲] noted the link between liberal democracy and freedom of the press and emphasized the symbolic importance of abolishing the Publishing Act in consolidating democracy in Taiwan (*Legislative Yuan Official Gazette* 1999a:44):

> I think there is a special significance to abolishing the Publishing Act. We can say that there is real democracy in Taiwan, that we are a free country. I hope that the whole nation can cherish democracy and freedom of speech and of thought and that we can make Taiwan into a real democracy that enjoys freedom of speech.

Again, any implicit or explicit references to Confucianism are absent from this discussion. Instead, the rationale for the repeal of the Publishing Act was rooted in standard democratic theory and universal human rights.

Gender Equality in Employment Act, 2002

While the 1947 Republic of China Constitution guaranteed equality before the law for all citizens of the Republic "irrespective of sex, religion, race, class, or party affiliation," the reality in Taiwan was that women faced both formal and informal discrimination. Women's rights organizations had begun to form even before the lifting of martial law in 1989, but the post-martial-law era saw those groups mushroom in both membership and political activism (Chang 2009: 146-149). The key gender-related piece of legislation that these organizations promoted was the Gender Equality in Employment Act [兩性工作平等法] (Council of Labor Affairs 2005). It took more than ten years from when it was first introduced as a draft bill in 1990 for the Act to be passed by the Legislative Yuan in 2001 and signed into law by the President in 2002. During that decade, the act went through several revisions and numerous debates. The final bill included the following key provisions: equal pay for equal work; the prohibition of discrimination on the basis of gender in hiring, promotion, and termination; the prevention of sexual harassment in the workplace; the establishment of parental leave policies; and the creation of the Commission on Gender Equality to investigate employers' misconduct.

Nothing in the legislative debate would suggest that Confucian values had anything to do with the passage of the bill. Neither the supporters nor the opponents of the bill laid claim to the Confucian tradition in making their particular case. Instead, the debate took place within a liberal framework, as the contending sides tried to determine the meaning and policy implications of equal rights and equal treatment as it related to women. One point of disagreement between the legislators was the issue of to whom the bill would eventually apply. Legislator Zhang Renxiang [章仁香], as an example, argued that members of the military, public officials, and teachers ought to be included in the law because "if I am working for the government and experience sexual harassment, I should have a channel in which to lodge a complaint" (*Legislative Yuan Official Gazette* 1999b:5). Legislator Lee Cheng-chong [李正宗] queried: "I do not know why the Executive Yuan would exclude the military, public officers, and teachers in this bill" (*Legislative Yuan Official Gazette* 1999b:6). The Executive Yuan's Director of the Council of Labor Affairs, Hong Ruey-Ching [洪瑞清] similarly stated that it was "an undeniable truth that problems [associated with] gender equality can happen in these workplaces, including the problem of sexual harassment," leading him to conclude that these occupations must be incorporated into the final bill (*Legislative Yuan Official Gazette* 1999b:7). The assumption behind such claims is a classical liberal one: no gender-specific occupation exists. Without any gender-specific roles, it makes no sense to limit the application of the law by occupation. Even those arguing for some limit on the bill's applicability hardly averred to a conservative, traditional Confucian argument that women are ill-suited to perform certain tasks. Instead, they simply countered that in some places men and women were treated differently, such as the military with its compulsory service for men, but not for women (even if women can enlist if they choose to). Nonetheless, the final bill stipulated that the Act is applicable to "public personnel, educational personnel, and military personnel" (chap. I, art. 2). The only proviso to that idea is that "if the nature of work is only suitable to a particular sex, the above restrictions shall not apply" (chap. II, art. 7). Little evidence exists, however, to suggest that this wording has been used to restrict the application of the law. Kuo Su-Chun [郭素春] spoke for many of her fellow members of the Legislative Yuan when she noted that "the purpose of establishing the Gender Equality in Employment Act is to insure that men and women can start their work on an equal footing and with the promise of equal treatment" (*Legislative Yuan Official Gazette* 1999b:6).

Aboriginal Basic Law, 2005

The indigenous people of Taiwan trace their lineage to a neolithic Austronesian group who first arrived on the island around four thousand B.C.E. (Davison and Reed 1998:4). Until the seventeenth century, Chinese immigration to Taiwan was minimal, which meant that Yuanzhumin dominated the island's political life (Wang 2001:10-12). Larger-scale immigration during the Qing dynasty (1683-1895), followed by Japanese control of Taiwan from 1895 to 1945 and the Nationalist takeover in 1947, dramatically changed the situation for indigenous Taiwanese. In their different ways, the Chinese during the Qing dynasty, the Japanese, and the KMT had little regard for the rights of indigenous people. From the standpoint of aborigines, each of these groups acted as colonial overlords who pursued policies that oppressed indigenous people, legislated them out of existence, or (in the best-case scenario) neglected them. During the Qing dynasty, for example, indigenous people, whom the Han regarded as barbarians, had to take a Han surname to be recognized as full persons and to operate within the Confucian state. Having gained political control of Taiwan, the KMT attempted to assimilate the Yuanzhumin by requiring the use of Mandarin in public schools rather than native languages, confiscating indigenous lands through the power of eminent domain, and promoting a sense of Chinese nationalism that negated the distinctive historical and cultural experiences of indigenous people (Mona 2007). Following the pattern established during the Qing dynasty, KMT authorities gave those aborigines who had yet officially to change their name three months to select a Chinese family name; those who could not or chose not to do so were given a name by a government bureaucrat (Wang 1994:25). The goal of these policies was the cultural assimilation of indigenous peoples; the result, intended or not, was the social, political, and economic marginalization of the Yuanzhumin who were and are disproportionately poor and undereducated (Rigger 1984:84-123).

The rise of a distinctive indigenous political movement in Taiwan coincided with the gradual democratization on the island throughout the 1980s and 1990s. Perhaps ironically, the Yuanzhumin have generally favored the "mainlander"-controlled KMT to the "native Taiwanese"-dominated Democratic Progressive Party. Not only have indigenous groups at times benefited from a patronage-based relationship with the KMT, but aborigines initially concluded, not without reason, that they had little in common with the "Taiwanese"-based ethnic nationalism of the DPP (Simon 2010:727). While KMT policy toward them was hardly progressive, at least initially, the connection with the KMT bore some fruit when the party-controlled National Assembly passed a law in 1994 that gave indigenous people the legal right to reclaim their traditional name. The following year the official name for aboriginals was changed from Shanbao (mountain compatriots [山胞]) to Yuanzhumin (indigenous inhabitants [原住民]), and in 1996 the Council of Indigenous People was promoted to a ministry-level rank within the Executive Yuan. The KMT also granted indigenous representatives set-aside seats in the Legislative Yuan, a process that was formalized with a 2005 Constitutional amendment reserving six seats for indigenous legislators. In 1994 and 2000 the Constitution was also revised to address some of the concerns of indigenous people. The 1947 Constitution had said nothing about indigenous groups, let alone their rights or the obligation of the state toward them. Under the most recent revision, the state must now actively "preserve and foster the development of aboriginal languages and cultures . . . safeguard the status and political participation of the aborigines . . . and provide assistance and encouragement for aboriginal education, culture . . . and social welfare." The article concludes by promising that the measures for insuring these principles "shall be established by law."

Simultaneously, indigenous groups began to flex their political muscles in the months leading up to the 2000 presidential election. Although they only represent 2 percent of the island's total population, in what looked to be a close election, the aboriginal vote could not be ignored. Indigenous organizations sent a letter to all the presidential candidates asking them to sign a new partnership agreement between the government and aborigines. Only DPP candidate Chen Shui-bian complied. His somewhat unexpected election raised the hopes of indigenous groups that the DPP would support laws granting them some form of political and legal autonomy (Simon 2010:727). In 2002, Chen again acknowledged the agreement with representatives of all recognized aboriginal peoples, and shortly after his reelection in 2004, the Executive Yuan finally proposed the Aboriginal Basic Law [原住民基本法] (see Lin 2000). The Act marked a decisive break from the assimilationist past by recognizing the autonomy of indigenous peoples on their designated territories, providing funds to develop indigenous languages, and prohibiting the forced removal of indigenous people from their land (United Nations High Commission for Refugees 2008).

The debate on the bill exhibited a fascinating interplay among the concerns of indigenous politicians about the motives and commitment of the government to indigenous rights, lingering ethnic tensions between the indigenous peoples and Han Chinese, and a strong commitment to liberal political norms. In response to a comment by a government official on the need for more time to work out the details of the bill, for example, KMT indigenous Representative Liao Kuo-Tung [廖國棟] rather sarcastically noted that "we [indigenous groups] are part of a New Partnership before the election, but we are supposed to just deal with it [the law] by ourselves after the election" (*Legislative Yuan Official Gazette* 2004:72). In a similar vein, Seediq national and non-partisan legislator Walis Pelin [瓦歷斯·貝林] complained that the government was now saying "the provisions are too complicated, and you suggest that the name of the bill is not appropriate. From my point of view, you seem anxious to impede the bill rather than pass it" (*Legislative Yuan Official Gazette* 2000:237). The Chair of the Executive Yuan's Council of Indigenous Peoples, Chen Chien-nien [陳建年], repeatedly tried to reassure supporters of the bill by suggesting that "the only way to establish the legislation" was through "communication and consultation," all of which took time (*Legislative Yuan Official Gazette* 2004:72).

A primary point of contention in the debate was on the issue of autonomy, or specifically how far the bill would go to establish territories under the political and legal control of aboriginal groups. On this point, the debate mirrored what one would find in countries such as Canada, Australia, Bolivia, or Mexico, all of which have grappled with the same policy question. As is often the case, opponents invariably made the *reductio ad absurdum* argument that allowing any territory to be genuinely autonomous opens the door to further claims of autonomy. To make his case that it is difficult to "return lands" to aborigines, DPP legislator Perng Shaw-Jiin [彭紹瑾] claimed that "if we want to deal with aboriginal land, then I suppose the entire island of Taiwan belongs to aborigines" (*Legislative Yuan Official Gazette* 2000:238). People First Party representative Tsai Chung-Han [蔡中涵] took the argument a step further when he suggested that "if we specify the rights of aborigines in this act, the Hakka will probably also ask us to pass a Hakka Basic Law" (*Legislative Yuan Official Gazette* 2000:245). Supporters of the bill, particularly those members who were indigenous themselves, invariably countered that the Han Chinese had manipulated Aborigines in the past and, without the right law in place, the Han would disadvantage them into the future. In the last version of the bill, the government changed a reference to "Aboriginal Autonomous Regions" to "Aboriginal Areas." Fearing that this step might signal a movement away from genuine autonomy for indigenous groups, Representative Liao noted: "If aboriginal regions are limit to 'Aboriginal Areas' or 'Autonomous Regions' without any basis in a legal document, I am afraid the aboriginal land will soon become the property of Han people. For four hundred years, aboriginal lands have been gradually occupied by the Han and by one government after another" (*Legislative Yuan Official Gazette* 2004:73-74). KMT indigenous legislator Tjivuluan [曾華德] evoked a similar concern: "Indigenous people will be seen as second-class citizens if the ruling party does not have a commitment to eliminating its Han chauvinism, even though we were masters of Taiwan until four hundred years ago" (*Legislative Yuan Official Gazette* 2000:240). At a particularly tense moment in the debate, KMT aboriginal representative Kao Yang-Sheng [高揚昇] even suggested that the "Han people move back to mainland China" (*Legislative Yuan Official Gazette* 2000:250).

Time and again the debate focused on the language, discourse, and rationale of ethnic politics and of human rights rather than the teachings of Confucius. DPP member and Taiwanese Premier Yu Shyi-kun [游錫堃] noted President Chen's commitment to "the ideals of human rights" and the "Charter of the United Nations" as it related to the rights of indigenous groups (*Legislative Yuan Official Gazette* 2004:74). Representative Walis Pelin similarly affirmed, "I support the Aboriginal Basic Law as a way to emphasize the human rights system. Today, the government of the Republic of China has been moving toward a modern state, and respect for human rights should be reflected in the law" (*Legislative Yuan Official Gazette* 2000:234). In short, to be a modern state is to promote human rights, in this case in the form of the rights of indigenous people. Member Kao hoped that the passage of the bill would "solve aboriginals' problems of not getting respect, social equity, and justice" (*Legislative Yuan Official Gazette* 2000:250), all of which are values central to contemporary liberal political regimes.

Even when the debate deviated from the language of liberalism and took on a more Taiwanese-focused theme, it was not Confucianism that entered the mix, but cross-strait relations. At one point, Premier Yu warned that the idea of a "state within a state doesn't mean another country. It means greater autonomy for aboriginal groups, but it doesn't mean that those regions have their own national defense or armies" (*Legislative Yuan Official Gazette* 2004:74). Perhaps in an effort to win greater sympathy from this DPP government official, Representative Liao hinted that autonomy for aboriginal groups might set an important precedent—a camel's nose under the proverbial tent—for Taiwan's political independence: "I hope the Premier can respect the aboriginal desire for their own nation. I want the Premier to know that in the future, if 'the Country of Takasago' [高砂國, an early name used by the Japanese emperor for Taiwan[2]] is really established, it will more easily be recognized by the United Nations as a member than the Republic of China or the Taiwan Republic would be" (*Legislative Yuan Official Gazette* 2004:74). Perhaps amused, Premier Yu countered, "Not really. We still have to see what China thinks about that" (*Legislative Yuan Official Gazette* 2004:74). In the end, virtually any political debate in Taiwan can eventually be reduced to its implications for relations with mainland China.

Conclusion

The legislative debate on democratization and human rights demonstrates clearly that western political values, rather than Confucian ones, were paramount. For the most part, Confucianism seemed irrelevant to both supporters and opponents of each of the four bills. The only plausible exception is when the KMT Ministry of the Interior hinted that democratization should progress along with such values as order, stability, and the pursuit of the national interest. How is it that a belief system such as Confucianism, which was and remains so important to East Asians, could have been ignored as Taiwan revolutionized its political institutions?

One argument is that, as Weber contended more than a century ago, Confucianism is itself inherently conservative, and any deviations from the status quo must necessarily abandon this ideology. These four bills that we have analyzed obviously were major departures from the political norm. In this account, therefore, one can easily understand why the debate turned on western notions of democracy, press freedom, and gender and indigenous rights.

But, a counter-reading exists. In this alternative interpretation, the DPP controlled the rhetoric of political liberalization and had already concluded that Confucianism was either of no help or even hostile to their agenda. Here, political context mattered. As we noted in previous chapters, the transmission of Confucianism led democracy advocates to this apparently reasonable conclusion. After all, the authoritarian state had manipulated this ideology to justify its violations of democratic rights. Given such a reality, it is hard to imagine that DPP leaders would have looked to the Confucian tradition for intellectual support. Instead, they embraced western liberal rationales for their positions. Despite the negative experience with Confucianism of this pioneering Tangwai generation of democracy activists and their corresponding rejection of the tradition, however, one should not necessarily conclude that their judgment of this belief system was accurate. Perhaps Confucianism is actually more amenable to democracy than they imagined. As the following chapter demonstrates, some political thinkers and activists in Taiwan have found ways to fuse liberal values with Confucian ones.

Notes

1. Although today's Legislative Yuan is the chief island-wide legislative body, before 2005 it shared power with the now-defunct National Assembly [國民大會]. Under the ROC Constitution, the National Assembly was supposed to make most constitutional-level decisions. Neither the Legislative Yuan nor the National Assembly, however, effectively checked executive power under martial law (Copper 2003:118-120; Roy 2003:82-85; Government Information Office 2009: Appendix III).

2. In 1593, Japanese Emperor Hideyoshi sent a letter to the leaders of the country he called "Takasago," ordering them to pay tribute to Japan. Takasago was today's Taiwan (Sansom 1961:378-379).

Chapter 6
Toward a Liberal-Democratic Confucianism: Evidence from Taiwan

The Master said "When the multitude hate a man, it is necessary to examine the case. When the multitude like a man, it is necessary to examine into the case."

Confucius (1971:302), *Analects* (XV. xxvii)

An examination of Chinese and Japanese history shows that rare indeed were the gentlemen of great talent and ability who were born at the right time. . . . Confucius was born before his time, and so was Mencius.

Fukuzawa (2008:68) Yukichi, *An Outline of a Theory of Civilization*

No better example for the potential of a nuanced rapprochement between Confucian and liberal democratic values could be found than the life and work of China's Chang Peng-Chun [張彭春]. Chang was a Confucian philosopher, did post-graduate studies with John Dewey, was the President of Nankai University, and served as the Vice-Chair of the Human Rights Commission that was responsible for drafting the Universal Declaration of Human Rights. In her memoirs about the Declaration, Eleanor Roosevelt recounted the following story about Chang:

> Dr. Chang was a pluralist and held forth in charming fashion on the proposition that there is more than one kind of ultimate reality. The Declaration, he said, should reflect more than simply Western ideas. . . . His remark, though addressed to Dr. Humphrey, was really directed at Dr. Malik, from whom it drew a prompt retort as he expounded at some length on the philosophy of Thomas Aquinas. . . . I remember that at one point Dr. Chang suggested that the Secretariat might well spend a few months studying the fundamentals of Confucianism!

By all accounts, Chang was among the most influential and active members of the eighteen-person Human Rights Commission (Glendon 1999; Waltz 2002). In that role, he offered insights from his particular Confucian background, but more significantly, Chang had a unique ability to communicate between cultural traditions in a way that allowed for genuine cross-cultural collaboration. He was faithful to the particularities of divergent views, while simultaneously being able to articulate the shared principles of human rights.

The results of our study offer evidence to support both sides of the debate on the compatibility between Confucianism and liberal-democratic values. The elites that we interviewed for the book have by and large concluded that Confucian values are irrelevant or even hostile to their efforts to promote democracy, gender rights, indigenous rights, and press freedom. As we noted in chapter 2, this negative view is partially explained by their political experiences. In particular, the KMT's propaganda that married the views of the authoritarian state with Confucian values sullied the tradition for later generations. The more recent attempt by the "Communist" government on mainland China to resuscitate a Confucian tradition it once reviled is predictably and understandably interpreted as the latest example of the political manipulation of Confucianism. Democratic leaders generally want no part of it. The former DPP presidential candidate and democracy activist, Peng Ming-min (2008), alluded to this idea when he said to us, "Of course, you can selectively quote all sorts of words from Confucius and make him a kind of democrat, or modern thinker. But that does not really mean that those who say those words are really democrats."

Confucianism as a state ideology has done much to mar the tradition, but more than political expediency explains why it is difficult to reconcile Confucianism and democracy. A number of political theorists, Chinese and western, have made persuasive arguments that Confucianism does not lend itself to democracy or the promotion of liberal-democratic values. Efforts to reconcile them, these theorists contend, inevitably distort what Confucianism actually teaches about politics. Li Chenyang (1997:187) writes that Confucianism, at least in its traditional form, "has no place for the concept of rights." Instead, he argues, "the primary concern for Confucianism has to do with duty, not liberty." Li implies that a focus on duty leaves little room for the idea of inalienable rights. David Elstein (2010) argues that the *Analects* offer a paternalistic vision of politics where virtuous rulers provide a model for good government based on their ethical behavior. The goal is to train political leaders to care about the common good. But the ideology remains a hierarchical, non-democratic vision that shows no interest in limiting state power and is ultimately a "government for the people, but not by the people" (2010:427). Hu Shaohua (1997) is only slightly less pessimistic when he concludes that "Confucianism is neither democratic nor antidemocratic," and "while [it is] not an insurmountable obstacle to democratization, it offers little help in that process."

Some formulations of particular Confucian values certainly do reduce respect for women, for example. In particular, traditional Confucianism's emphasis on social harmony seems to be hindering individual Taiwanese women's efforts to advance gender equality. One can certainly also understand how traditional Confucianism's inordinate deference to authority would run counter to the liberal principle that each human being has the right to equal political influence and is equally capable of political rationality. Assuming that only scholars or men may rule similarly violates this central democratic tenet. Equally problematic is the presumption that only the politically powerful may articulate the meaning of Confucianism. Our own empirical analysis, moreover, confirms that believing in some Confucian values diminishes support for women's rights.

Daniel Bell (2006; 2008) offers a number of intriguing insights on the theoretical compatibility of Confucianism with western-style, majoritarian liberal democracy. Bell rightly notes that much of the Asian-values literature offers a false choice between East Asian societies' abandoning their commitment to Confucian values in order to embrace western democratic ones and maintaining their fidelity to Confucianism at the expense of liberal democracy. In fact, this narrative was precisely the one explicitly or implicitly embraced by many of the Taiwanese democracy activists we interviewed. However, it is no more reasonable to think that East Asian societies will or ought to abandon their Confucian values any more than it is right to anticipate that the West will reject its Judeo-Christian heritage. Consequently, the struggle to promote human rights, Bell argues, can only be won "if it is fought in ways that build on, rather than challenge, local cultural traditions" (2006:65). Moreover, Bell affirms that Confucianism can contribute to any number of contemporary social and political issues. Specifically, he makes a convincing case that the application of Confucian teaching on just and unjust wars "has the potential to play the role of constraining China's imperial ventures overseas" (2008:35). He even suggests that stressing Confucian values can expand our notion of rights. An emphasis on filial piety, Bell demonstrates, has led many East Asian countries to pass laws that require children to provide financial support for their elderly parents (2006:77). Thus, the rights of the elderly are arguably more strongly protected and affirmed in East Asian countries than in the United States. Finally, Bell makes an important contribution by noting that political, religious, and cultural ideologies have distinctive historical pedigrees. It would be naïve in the extreme to presume that Confucianism is anything but East Asian in this historical sense, just as the historical roots of liberal democracy are predominantly western. As a consequence, Bell asks the right question when he wonders "is it really appropriate to uphold standards of human rights derived from the Western experience in East Asian societies?" (2008:9).

We part company with Bell on two key points, however. First, Bell offers a Sino-centric (or even more accurately, a mainland Sino-centric) focus. "The moral of the story," Bell informs his readers, "is that a creative adaptation of the legacy [Confucianism] can be helpful in dealing with the challenges of contemporary China" (2008:xiii). The primary challenge he has in mind is a crisis of legitimacy faced by China's rulers with the demise of Marxist-Leninist ideology, a void that Bell thinks can usefully and creatively be filled by Confucianism. From the standpoint of many Taiwanese activists, however, such a claim will be seen as little more than the manipulation of Confucianism for the Communist state's self-serving ends. Confucianism as an ideology loses credibility the more the Chinese state embraces it, which helps to explain why many Taiwanese advocates of democracy and human rights have turned to western values to promote their political agenda. A second concern we have with Bell's analysis is his suggestion that the idea of human rights will necessarily take a different form in East Asian societies because they are Confucian. He writes (2006: 73):

> [I]t is possible that most politically relevant actors, both officials and intellectuals, in East Asian societies typically endorse a somewhat different set of fundamental human goods than their counterparts in Western societies now and for the foreseeable future. . . . [I]t may mean that some Western conceptions of human rights are actually culturally specific conceptions of fundamental human goods, not readily accepted elsewhere.

The devil is in the proverbial details in such a claim: which human rights are culturally specific and therefore not transferable to different cultural contexts? Similarly, Bell juxtaposes "western" and "Confucian" notions of political legitimacy (Jiang and Bell 2012; Jiang 2012). But at a minimum, such assertions imply that some category of political values recognized as universal in the West is fundamentally incompatible with core Confucian principles. Yet evidence from this book suggests that the perceived relationship between Confucianism and democracy is, in fact, shifting, and that the supposed gap between "western" and "Confucian" understandings of human rights is disappearing.

To put these arguments in the context of this book, we note that the claim that Confucianism is hostile to democracy follows in the tradition of Weber's work on Confucianism. As we documented in the first chapter, Weber viewed Confucianism as a conservative, state-legitimating ideology. In contrast with Protestantism, Confucianism in his opinion could not support capitalist development or challenge authoritarian political practices. Weber had an essentially static understanding of the Confucian tradition. However, he also understood that ideologies are always evolving, and as a consequence, it is problematic to reify any single interpretation of the tradition as normative. Christianity, as an example, was dynamic, and the emergence of capitalism owed much to the development of a Protestant ethic within the larger Christian tradition. From a Weberian perspective, the question is whether such dynamism can exist within Confucianism. Again, this book indicates that the relationship between Confucianism and democracy is indeed evolving.

The mass-level data present an interesting picture. As we demonstrated in chapters 1 and 3, respondents in authoritarian and democratic states differ in how they appropriate Confucian and democratic values. Data from interviewees in authoritarian China and Singapore were more likely to exhibit a negative correlation between adherence to Confucian norms and support for key democratic values than were the responses from residents of democratic South Korea and Taiwan. What this result suggests is that whatever classical Confucianism "actually" teaches about political institutions and values, context matters a great deal for how people actually use and understand the tradition. A few of the political elites that we interviewed for our book have also begun to think in such terms.

While many democracy and human-rights activists in Taiwan believe that the Confucian tradition has been unhelpful in the past, some of them are ready to imagine that a reconstituted, less "fundamentalist" Confucianism could conceivably reinforce liberal-democratic values in the future. Legislator Kung Wen-chi (2008) highlighted one Confucian value that was potentially quite helpful in his work for aboriginal rights: "Confucius said that every man should be educated equally, without regard to a person's race. This is the important idea of nondiscrimination." Tsai Jen-chien (2008), former mayor of Hsinchu City and a democracy activist, was even more explicit in perceiving a possible union of Confucian and democratic values:

> If we understand the underlying features of Confucianism and democracy, they don't necessarily conflict with each other. It is not so much that Confucianism has facilitated democracy in Taiwan, but rather that Confucianism and democratic culture have learned to accommodate themselves to each other.

Democracy and women-rights activist Fan Yun (2008) likewise hints at a possible rapprochement between Confucianism and gender rights:

> It is the same for Confucianism as it is for Christianity. You have to reinterpret the Bible so that it can be understood for today. Perhaps the idea of junzi [君子] can be interpreted in a gender-neutral way, so that it is not simply the "noble man" idea.

At least some pioneers in the island's democratization movement, then, have not completely given up hope on this ancient Chinese ideology.

One Confucianism practitioner that we interviewed, moreover, is even more optimistic. Wang Tsai-Kuei (2008; see also Hwang 2008; Lee Ching-Shang 2008), who coordinates and teaches in a network of private schools devoted to the Chinese classics, similarly implies that the historical manipulation of Confucianism by authoritarian political leaders does not preclude its viability as a basis for democratic values. "The ancient Chinese did not establish a democratic system," he admits, but "if Confucius were alive today, he would support democracy." In his view, "Confucianism did not lead to a kind of democracy earlier because no democratic structure existed then." Though "Confucianism always promoted the idea of taking care of people," the time was not yet right to form a democracy. For Wang, "Confucianism, democracy, and human rights are completely compatible." In fact, he argues, "Confucian morality forms an even better foundation for human rights than western thought does." In contrast to anchoring rights in an overly idealistic, western view of human nature, "Confucianism produces even more respect for human beings by using ren (benevolent empathy)." Even a "bad person can become a good person by learning about goodness." Thus, human beings infused with ren would refrain from using torture or other non-democratic means to achieve their political goals because they could imagine what it would be like to be tortured or otherwise abused themselves. According to this promoter of Confucianism, the ideology also instills a "conscience" in people that is later useful in practical politics: "If a person had no conscience and learned democracy, the result would be a sham democracy" of endless partisan bickering. "There is no real democracy if people are only fighting for the benefit of their own particular party," instead of seeking the

good of everyone. "If all [political] parties in Taiwan had taught all of the Confucian values in the schools since 1949," he concludes, "democracy in Taiwan
would be much better now."

At the post-secondary-school level, moreover, professors and other scholars
based in Taiwan have been at work constructing a Confucian justification for
democracy and various human rights. In contrast to many liberal theorists who
wish to found Asian democracy on the "complete westernization" of Chinese-
speaking societies, the mainlander Taiwanese philosopher Mou Zongsan (牟宗
三) contended that some elements of the Confucian tradition (e.g., "zhengtong"
[政統]) could form the basis for political freedom and self-determination (Mou
1968-1969; Mou 2003:16-19; Clower 2010:41; see also Tamney and Chiang
2002). Mou's political and intellectual ally Xu Fuguan [徐復觀] similarly held
that the originally pro-democratic Confucianism of the pre-Qin era became
distorted by the authoritarianism of the Han and later dynasties. Yet at base, Xu
believed, the ideology's assumption that humans were fundamentally good
(xingshan lun [性善論]) suggested that people should be allowed to govern
themselves (Xu 1979; Chen 2009). More recently, Lee Ming-huei [李明輝]
(2005:33-70 & 95-96) has further developed Mou's and Xu's line of thought,
deepening our understanding of the political implications of the Confucian view
of human nature and the idea that people form the foundation for government
(minben [民本]). Tan Yuan-ping (2004:103-119), another Taiwanese academic,
has similarly argued that Confucian ren implies both political equality and true
(as opposed to coerced) harmony between citizens and the government.
Taiwanese scholars Huang Chün-chie [黃俊杰] and Wu Kuang-ming [吳光明]
(1994:71) even go so far as to suggest that "Confucianism is a philosophy of
unconditional reverence for the autonomous individual in all dimensions."

"On the ground" evidence also exists for a marrying of the Confucian and
liberal-democratic traditions. In his 2007 study, Richard Madsen analyzes the
development of four popular religious movements in Taiwan: Tzu Chi,
Buddha's Light Mountain, Dharma Drum Mountain, and the Enacting Heaven
Temple. He discovers that these Buddhist and Daoist organizations have
facilitated the democratic transition in Taiwan through their revival and
reinterpretation of Confucian values. Madsen shows that a Confucian moral
discourse remains central for each of the groups, yet the emphasis on a key
Confucian concept like the five right relationships has changed. Where once the
five lun might have meant deference to traditional authorities, they are now
understood to imply the complementary obligations among different people. For
Madsen, this change does not represent religious elites' rejection of "traditional"
norms but rather a revision of these principles "in light of evolving
circumstances" (2007:121).

Our results on the empirical relationship between support for Confucianism
and aboriginal rights suggest a similar evolution. As we noted in chapter 3, two
of the three Confucian values (family loyalty and social hierarchies) had no effect on attitudes toward aboriginal rights, while the remaining value of social
harmony increased support for Yuanzhumin. This finding is surprising and has

important ramifications for the rights of Yuanzhumin and for liberal democracy more generally. Confucianism is often perceived as promoting the superiority of Han Chinese. Key passages from Confucian texts endorse that idea, and the repeated attempts by Han Chinese to wipe out Yuanzhumin culture and to promote Confucian values reinforced this message. Given such a history, one would expect that Confucianism would be absolutely incompatible with the political and cultural rights of native peoples. That Confucian values do not undermine support for indigenous peoples, however, suggests that the tradition is malleable and can be interpreted in a way that advances the rights of Yuanzhumin. In one historical context, the Confucian value of social harmony, for example, was interpreted to mean that those who were not Han needed to assimilate to Confucian values in order to be fully included within the political community. In a different political environment, however, social harmony is apparently understood to require a respect for the rights and practices of different cultural groups. This particular Confucian value thus seems to have been transformed by democratization. In the final analysis, what a tradition actually "means" is mediated through political and cultural practices that both shape, and are shaped by, the tradition. Confucianism does not inherently support or oppose the rights of Yuanzhumin; rather, the concrete meaning of this ideology depends entirely on who is interpreting and applying the tradition.

The history of Christianity in the West illustrates how a deeply rooted ideology is malleable over time. During different periods, both Protestant and Catholic churches opposed political and economic liberalism (Kalyvas 1996; Gould 1999). The Roman Catholic Church, in particular, took several centuries to make its peace with such ideas as majoritarian rule, civil liberties, and church-state separation. After listing a number of "errors" of modern thought, including the idea that the church ought to be separated from the state, Pope Pius IX (2012) famously concluded his 1864 Syllabus of Errors with his denial that "the Roman Pontiff, can, and ought to, reconcile himself, and come to terms with progress, liberalism, and modern civilization." Given such a position, it was hardly inevitable that the Catholic Church would embrace political liberalism, but that is precisely what the church did over the next century. The Church did so by redirecting its focus to those parts of the Christian tradition that supported such fundamental principles as individual rights and democracy. It was not so much a question of the Church abandoning Catholic principles, as allowing them to evolve in light of changing circumstances. The notion that the Catholic Church could simultaneously retain foundational commitments and evolve is nicely captured in the title of John Noonan's book (2005), *A Church that Can and Cannot Change.* We believe that Confucianism also contains many intellectual resources that enable it to be reconfigured in a democratic direction, both to change and not change.

The issue for us is not so much whether these theoretical interpretations or on-the-ground revisions are fully consistent with every aspect of the Confucianism espoused by the movement's founders Kongzi (Confucius) and Mengzi (Mencius). Instead, our concern is more empirical: are people in Taiwan at the mass and the elite level finding ways to reinterpret the inherited tradition in ways that can embrace democratic values? The answer is clearly "yes."

Moreover, a number of Confucian values could be used to temper the excesses of western-style democracy and individualism. Confucianism's communal ethos recognizes the most salient intermediary institution, the extended family, which binds human beings together into a meaningful community. Likewise, the stress on social harmony can serve as a valuable check on the tendency in some forms of political liberalism toward the prioritization of individual rights with no thought to the social and cultural context through which those rights can be expressed. Finally, filial piety might help individuals see beyond their narrow self-interest to embrace obligations they have to previous generations.

Perhaps what is emerging in Taiwan is the privatization of Confucianism, or at least its formal separation from the state. This development is unique in the tradition's history since state Confucianism was the norm for many centuries and may well have undermined the credibility of the ideology. As former President Lee Teng-hui (2008) noted in his interview with us, "When political rulers dominated countries by using Confucianism, people in those countries probably did not really believe in it." Even the more contemporary history of greater China has been one of manipulation of Confucianism by both the KMT during its authoritarian phase in Taiwan and more recently by Communist officials on the mainland. In this regard, David Elstein (2010:432) suggests that a Confucianism that is "relegated to personal ethical values" would have "little political impact." He might be right if the standard for judgment is state Confucianism, but the decoupling of Confucianism from the state does not necessarily weaken the doctrine's political impact. As Alexis de Tocqueville noted nearly two centuries ago, religion in America did not directly involve itself in government, yet it was "the first of their political institutions" (Tocqueville 1969:292). The effect of religion in America, he contended, was indirect; political parties were not organized around religion and religious officials played no formal part in government. Yet, religious values infused people's lives and made possible democratic governance. It might similarly be said for Taiwan that the indirect, long-term political effects of Confucianism may be as significant as the direct effects Confucianism assumed in earlier eras.

Is Taiwan a harbinger of things to come in mainland China, a country that is similarly Confucian and set to become the world's largest economy, but that has yet to make the transition to democracy? The answer might be negative if the Taiwanese case is so unique that one cannot generalize about the island beyond its shores. Taiwan is quickly developing a national identity that plays on the island's cultural and historical distinctiveness (Brown 2004; Ku 2005). For example, the narrative about aboriginal rights increasingly highlights the anthropological facts that the Taiwanese Yuanzhumin are not Han Chinese, that they have been living on Taiwan for thousands of years, and that they have distinctive cultural practices that can be identified and promoted. Similarly, Taiwanese take understandable pride in their successful democratization, a process that distinguishes them from their mainland counterparts. Those factors might argue against generalizing from the Taiwanese experience to mainland China and other East Asian countries. But, one could point to an equal number of reasons to believe that Taiwan is not so unique and that its history can be replicated elsewhere. If Taiwan becomes a model, moreover, it will be in large part because of a capacity to marry the eastern, Confucian tradition with the western, liberal one in a way that is faithful to both.

Democracy and Confucian values are not incompatible, but neither is a marrying of these perspectives inevitable. If history is any judge, political leaders will manipulate Confucian values for the leaders' self-interested purposes; we can only hope that citizens will offer counter-interpretations that highlight the more democratically inclined features of the tradition.

Glossary of Non-English Terms

benshengren (本省人, Mandarin): "people from this province," or ethnically Fujianese or Hakka "native Taiwanese" whose ancestors migrated to Taiwan before 1949

cai-te-lang (在地人, Taiwanese/Hokkien): "people from this land," see *benshengren*

Chen (陳, Mandarin): small vassal state of ancient China during the Zhou dynasty, located in present-day Henan province

Chu (楚, Mandarin): initially small but expanding state of ancient China during the Zhou dynasty, near today's Hubei province

dajia gongzhi, heping gongsheng (大家共治，和平共生, Mandarin): roughly "everyone will govern together, and public peace will ensue"

Dharma (धर्म, Sanskrit): idea of natural law or duty in south-Asian religious thought, teachings of the Buddha

er-er-ba (二二八, Mandarin): massacre of 2-28, or February 28, 1947, in Taiwan

Hakka (客家, Hakka): ethnic minority and its language in Taiwan and southern China, noted for their history of migration and political leadership

Han (漢, Mandarin): majority ethnic group in Chinese society

Ilha Formosa (Portuguese): "beautiful island," name given to Taiwan by early Portuguese explorers

Joseon (조선, Korean): name for Korea and of longest-running Korean dynasty from fifteenth to nineteenth centuries

junzi (君子, Mandarin): "gentleman," or virtuous man in Confucian thought

Kongzi (孔子, Mandarin): Confucius

linzhang (臨長, Mandarin): government or party official responsible for a particular urban neighborhood

Lu (魯, Mandarin): small vassal state of ancient China during the Zhou dynasty, located in today's Shandong province

lun (倫, Mandarin): human "relationship," five pairs of which lie at the heart of Confucian social ethics

Mengzi (孟子, Mandarin): Mencius

minben (民本, Mandarin): "people as the foundation," Confucian idea that rulers only succeed if they enjoy the support of the people

Nankai (南開, Mandarin): literally "southern opening," name of mainland Chinese university today in Tianjin

nüzi (女子, Mandarin): women or girls

qi (器, Mandarin): utensil

Qing (清, Mandarin): last dynasty of China from 1644 to 1911, replaced after Sun Yat-sen's Republican revolution

reductio ad absurdum (Latin): "reducing to the absurd," countering an argument by noting its most extreme implication

ren (仁, Mandarin): a key Confucian virtue, benevolent empathy, humaneness, or love for others

Shanbao (山胞, Mandarin): "mountain compatriots," condescending name used for indigenous Taiwanese before democratization

Shuo Yuan (說苑, Mandarin): collection of originally oral, semi-fictional Chinese stories, often with a particular moral

Song (宋, Mandarin): name of major Chinese dynasty that lasted from 960 to 1279 C.E.

Sungkyunkwan (성균관 [成均館], Korean): roughly "Institute for Achievement in All Subjects," name of major Korean university founded in 1398

Taida (台大, Mandarin): short form for National Taiwan University, Taipei

Takasago (高砂國, Japanese): early Japanese name for Taiwan

Tangwai (黨外, Wade-Giles transcription of Mandarin), those "outside the party," non-KMT politicians and activists during the early phase of democratization who later became the Democratic Progressive Party

Tiananmen (天安門, Mandarin): "Gate of Heavenly Peace," most important public square in central Beijing and site of the massacre of pro-democracy students and their supporters on the night of June 3-4, 1989

Tzu Chi (慈濟, Wade-Giles transcription of Mandarin): "kind aid," Taiwan-based, Buddhist relief organization

waishengren (外省人, Mandarin): "people from outside of this province," or post-1949 mainlanders in Taiwan

xingshan lun (性善論, Mandarin): "doctrine of good nature," Confucian assumption that humans are fundamentally good

Yeungfaan (洋番, Cantonese): "Western/foreign barbarian," term of abuse used in nineteenth-century southeastern China to refer to ethnic Europeans

Yuan (院, Mandarin): "court," or branch of government in Republic of China according to Sun Yat-sen's political framework

Yuanzhumin (原住民; Mandarin): "original inhabitants," or indigenous/aboriginal Taiwanese

zhengtong (政統, Mandarin): "political tradition" in Confucianism, historical practice of interpreting Confucian principles to give them political implications

Zhongzheng (中正, Mandarin): roughly "central and upright," one of the "first names" of Chiang Kai-shek and now a district in central Taipei hosting the Chiang Kai-shek Memorial Hall

Ziyou shibao (自由時報, Mandarin): *Liberty Times*, a major pan-green daily newspaper in Taiwan and the sister publication of the English-language *Taipei Times*

Statistical Appendix

TABLE A3.1

Regression Models of Effect of Three Confucian Values
on Support for Liberal Democracy in 1995

	Democratization	Freedom of Speech	Women's Rights
Predictors			
Family Loyalty	.060	-.079	-.246*
Social Hierarchies	-.165	-.128	-.063
Social Harmony	-.044	-.247	-.193*
Income	-.009	-.008	-.001
Education	.076*	-.033	.041
Female	-.359*	-.462*	.078
Age	.006	.003	.001
Mainlander	.214	-.020	.528*
Yuanzhumin	.046	.170	-.463*
Other Ethnicity	-.385	.372	.188
Urbanicity	.177*	-.010	-.132*
Christian	.835*	.219	-.340
Not Religious	.167	.312	.296*
Single	.309	.370	.488*
N	609	660	647
R^2 (Nagelkerke)/R^2	.079	.044	.134
χ^2		18.731*	
df.		14	

Notes: Data from Taiwan subset of 1995 World Values Survey. Equations for Democratization and Women's Rights estimated using ordinary-least-squares regression, while equation for Freedom of Speech estimated with dichotomous logit. All regressors are dummy variables except for Democratization (range = 6 to 16), Women's Rights (3 to 11), Family Loyalty (1 to 4), Social Hierarchies (1 to 3), Social Harmony (1 to 3), Income (1 to 10), Education (1 to 8), Age (20 to 75), and Urbanicity (4 to 8).
*$p < .05$

Statistical Appendix

TABLE A3.2
Regression Models of Effect of Three Confucian Values on Support for Liberal Democracy in 2001 and 2009

	Democrati- zation	Freedom of Speech	Women's Rights	Indigenous Rights
Predictors				
Family Loyalty	.277*	-.085*	.361*	-.071
Social Hierarchies	-.206	-.046	-.081	.061
Social Harmony	-.157	.026	-.452*	.183*
Income	.115	.045*	-.061	-.024
Education	.102*	-.007	.172*	.175*
Female	-.087	.047	.434*	-.154
Age	.013	-.007*	-.004	-.002
Mainlander	-.207	-.039	-.003	.098
Yuanzhumin/	.392	-.177	-.608	
%Yuanzhumin				-.043*
Other Ethnicity	-.080	-.127	.360	-.391
Urbanicity	-.001	.022	.037	
Urban				.026
Christian	.030	-.016	.540*	
Not Religious	-.119	.102	.017	
Single	.228	-.004	.019	.167
N	995	1037	1169	751
R^2 (Nagelkerke)/R^2	.084	.043	.103	.037
χ^2			100.484*	25.298*
df.			14	12

Notes: Data from Taiwan subset of 2001 Asian Barometer (columns 1-3) and 2009 TNS Taiwan Aborigines Study. Data for column 4 weighted by gender, age, and region. Equations for Democratization and Freedom of Speech estimated using ordinary-least-squares regression, while equations for Women's Rights and Indigenous Rights estimated with ordered logit. All regressors are dummy variables except for Democratization (range = 5 to 17), Freedom of Speech (2 to 8), Women's Rights (1 to 4), Family Loyalty (1 to 4 for cols. 1-3; 1 to 5 for col. 4), Social Hierarchies (1 to 4 for cols. 1-3; 1 to 5 for col. 4), Social Harmony (1 to 4 for cols. 1-3; 1 to 5 for col. 4), Income (1 to 5 for cols. 1-3; 2 to 16 for col. 4), Education (1 to 10 for cols. 1-3; 1 to 5 for col. 4), Age (21 to 89 for cols. 1-3; 15 to 64 for col. 4), %Yuanzhumin (0.17 to 29.54 for col. 4), Urbanicity (1 to 8 for cols. 1-3).
*p < .05

Bibliography

Interviews and Personal Communication

Calivat Gadu [鐘興華; Director, Council of Indigenous Peoples [原住民族委員會], Executive Yuan[行政院]]. 2008. Personal interview, May 5, Taipei.

Chang Po-Ya [張博雅; President, Chia-Yi City Community University [嘉義市社區大學] and former Mayor, Chiayi City]. 2008. Personal interview, May 13, Chiayi.
_____. 2012. E-mail message, May 15, Chiayi.

Chen Man-Li [陳曼麗; President, National Alliance of Taiwan Women's Associations [台灣婦女團體全國聯合會]]. 2008. Personal interview, May 19, Taipei.

Chen Mingyu [陳明玉; Chinese Language Teacher, Taipei Municipal Zhongzheng Senior High School [台北市立中正高級中學]. 2008. Personal interview, May 22, Taipei.

Chen Yi-Wen Evelyn [陳怡文; Policy Analyst, Amnesty International Taiwan]. 2008. Personal interview, May 26, Taipei.

Fan Yun [范雲; Assistant Professor of Sociology, National Taiwan University [國立台灣大學] and Chair [董事長], Board of Directors, Awakening Foundation [婦女新知基金會]]. 2008. Personal interview, May 16, Taipei.

Goldin, Paul R. [Professor of Chinese Thought and Chair, Department of East Asian Languages and Civilizations, University of Pennsylvania]. 2011. E-mail message, December 28, Philadelphia, PA.

Hsu Tain-Tsair [許添財; Mayor, Tainan City, and democracy activist]. 2008. Personal interview, May 12, Tainan.

Huang Shuisheng [黃水勝; KMT Linzhang, Longsheng [龍生] district]. 2008. Personal interview, May 2, Taipei.

Huang Yi Jun [黃意君; Chief Editor, News Bureau, cti television [中天電視]]. Personal interview, May 19, Taipei.

Hwang Shyh-bin [黃世賓; legal assistant [助理], Taipei Regional Court [台北地方法院]]. 2008. Personal interview, May 19, Taipei.

Kao Yu-Chih [高毓智; Chair, Department of Policy and International Participation, National Alliance of Taiwan Women's Associations [台灣婦女團體全國聯合會]]. 2008. Personal interview, May 19, Taipei.

Kung Wen-chi [孔文吉; Yuanzhumin Member (KMT) of Legislative Yuan [立法院]]. 2008. Personal interview, May 5, Taipei.

Kuo Chen-Lung [郭崇倫; Deputy Editor-in-Chief, *China Times* [中國時報]]. 2008. Personal interview, May 15, Taipei.

Lee Ching-Shan [李清山; Public Relations Officer, Cultural Heritage Section [文化資產科], Department of Culture and Tourism [文化觀光處], Tainan City Government]. 2008. Personal interview, May 21, Tainan.

Lee Teng-hui [李登輝; former President, Republic of China]. 2008. Personal interview, May 16, Taipei.

Lin Fuxiong [林富雄; nonpartisan Linzhang, Zhongzheng [中正] district]. 2008. Personal interview, May 2, Taipei.

Liu Jeng Ming [劉正鳴; Principal, Taipei Municipal Zhongzheng Senior High School [台北市立中正高級中學]]. 2008. Personal interview, May 22, Taipei.

Miao Shulan [謀淑蘭; Chinese Language Teacher, Taipei Municipal Zhongzheng Senior High School [台北市立中正高級中學]]. 2008. Personal interview, May 22, Taipei.

Pasuya Poiconu [浦忠成; Director, National Museum of Prehistory [國立台灣史前文化博物館]]. 2008. Personal interview, May 10, Chiayi.

Peng Ming-min [彭明敏; former DPP presidential candidate and democracy activist]. 2008. Personal interview, May 21, Taipei.

Slingerland, Edward [Canada Research Chair in Chinese Thought and Embodied Cognition, Department of Asian Studies, University of British Columbia]. 2011. E-mail message, December 29, Vancouver, BC.

Tsai Chi-hsun [蔡季勳; Secretary-General, Taiwan Association for Human Rights [台灣人權促進會]]. 2008. Personal interview, May 22, Taipei.

Tsai Jen-chien [蔡仁堅; former Mayor, Hsinchu City, and democracy activist]. 2008. Personal interview, May 3, Hsinchu.

Tzou Jiing-wen [鄒景雯; Deputy Editor-in-Chief, Political News Bureau, *Liberty Times* [自由時報]]. 2008. Personal interview, May 14, Taipei.

Wang Tsai-Kuei [王財貴; Director, Taipei City International Educational Foundation for the Study of the Classics [台北市全球讀經教育基金會]]. 2008. Personal interview, May 23, Taipei.

Wu, Tim E. M. [吳英明; Director General, Bureau of Human Resource Development [公教人力發展局], Kaohsiung City Government, and Professor of Political Economy, National Sun Yat-sen University [國立中山大學]]. 2008. Personal interview, May 12, Kaohsiung.

Yang Gin-Huey [楊景卉; Executive Secretary, Amnesty International Taiwan]. 2008. Personal interview, May 26, Taipei.

Yu Jy-Haw [尤之浩; Chief, Ophthalmology Department, Taipei City Hospital [台北市立聯合醫院], and former Section Chief, Department of Health [衛生署], Executive Yuan [行政院]]. 2008. Personal interview, May 15, Taipei.

Print, Archival, Media, and Internet Sources

Abadi, Cameron. 2011. "Parliamentary Funk: The United States Isn't the Only Country Whose Legislature Doesn't Work." *Foreign Policy*, July 20, 14-18.

Ackerly, Brooke A. 2005. "Is Liberalism the Only Way Toward Democracy? Confucianism and Democracy." *Political Theory* 33(4):437-576.

Ackerly, Brooke A., and Wei Li. 2008. "What May Confucianism Offer? A Feminist View of Contemporary Structural Changes in China." Paper prepared for delivery for the Annual Meeting of the American Political Science Association, Boston.

Adams, Jonathan. 2008. "Taiwan's Indigenous People Try to Maintain Their Culture in and Ever Changing World." *Taiwan News*, May 4, 4.

Almond, Gabriel A., and Sidney Verba, 1963. *Civic Culture: Political Attitudes and Democracy in Five Nations.* Princeton: Princeton University Press.

Angle, Stephen. 2010. "Confucianism on the Comeback." *Social Education* 74(1):24-27.

Barr, Michael D. 2000. "Lee Kuan Yew and the 'Asian Values' Debate." *Asian Studies Review* 24(3):309-334.

Bell, Daniel A. 2006. *Beyond Liberal Democracy: Political Thinking for an East Asian Context.* Princeton: Princeton University Press.

_____. 2008. *China's New Confucianism: Politics and Everyday Life in a Changing Society.* Princeton: Princeton University Press.

Bellows, Thomas J. 1970. *The People's Action Party of Singapore: Emergence of a dominant Party System.* New Haven, CT: Yale University Southeast Asia Studies Center.

_____. 2003. *The Republic of China Legislative Yuan: A Study of Institutional Evolution.* Baltimore: Maryland Series in Contemporary Asian Studies, School of Law, University of Maryland.

Blundell, David, ed. 2012. *Taiwan Since Martial Law: Society, Culture, Politics, Economy.* Taipei: National Taiwan University Press.

Bo Yang. 1992. *The Ugly Chinamen and the Crisis of Chinese Culture.* Don J. Cohn and Jing Qing, eds. and trans. Saint Leonards, N.S.W., Australia: Allen & Unwin.

Boix, Carles. 2003. *Democracy and Redistribution.* Cambridge: Cambridge University Press.

Brown, Melissa J. 2004. *Is Taiwan Chinese? The Impact of Culture, Power, and Migration on Changing Identities.* Berkeley: University of California Press.

Central News Agency. 2008. "Taiwan's Press Freedom Rated Highest in East Asia." *Taiwan News*, May 1, 2.

Chan, Joseph. 1999. "A Confucian Perspectives on Human Rights for Contemporary China." Pp. 212-237 in Joanne R. Bauer and Daniel A. Bell, eds. *The East Asian Challenge for Human Rights.* Cambridge: Cambridge University Press.

Chang, Doris T. 2009. *Women's Movements in Twentieth-Century Taiwan.* Urbana: University of Illinois Press.

Chang Fu-chung [張富忠] and Chiu Wan-hsin [邱萬興]. 2005. *Lüse niandai: Taiwan minzhu yundong 25 nian* [綠色年代：台灣民主運動 25 年/Green Era: 25 Years of Taiwan's Democracy Movement]. 2 vols. Taipei: Caituan faren lüse lüxing wenjiao jijinhui.

Chang Yen-hsien [張炎憲] et al. 2004. Li Denghui xiansheng yu Taiwan minzhuhua [李登輝先生與台灣民主化/Mr. Lee Teng-hui and Taiwan's Democratization]. Taipei: Yushan she.

Chang Yu-tzung and Chu Yun-han. 2008. "How Citizens View Taiwan's New Democracy." Pp. 83-113 in Chu Yun-han, Larry Diamond, Andrew J. Nathan, and Doh Chull Shin, eds. *How East Asians View Democracy.* New York: Columbia University Press.

_____, _____, and Frank Tsai, 2005. "Confucianism and Democratic Values in Three Chinese Societies." *Issues & Studies* 41(4):1-33.

Chao, Linda, and Roman H. Myers. 2003. *The First Chinese Democracy: Political Life in the Republic of China on Taiwan.* Baltimore: Johns Hopkins University Press.

Chen, Albert H. Y. 2007. "Is Confucianism Compatible with Liberal Constitutional Democracy?" *Journal of Chinese Philosophy* 34(2):194-216.

_____. 2009. "Three Political Confucianisms and Half a Century." Unpublished paper, University of Hong Kong Faculty of Law. Available at http://papers.ssrn.com/sol3/papers.cfm?abstract_id=1366582 (accessed March 13, 2012).

Chen Chun-Kai [陳君愷]. 2004. *Taiwan "minzhu wenhua" fazhan shi yanjiu* [台灣「民主文化」發展史研究/Research on the Historical Development of Taiwan's "Democratic Culture"]. Taipei: Jiyi gongcheng.

Cheng Tun-jen. 2001. "Transforming Taiwan's Economic Structure in the 20th Century." Pp. 19-36 in Richard Louis Edmonds and Steven M. Goldstein, eds. *Taiwan in the Twentieth Century: A Retrospective View.* Cambridge: Cambridge University Press.

Chi Chan-nan [紀展南]. 2007. *Jiayi mazu po: Xu Shixian chuaqi* [嘉義媽組婆：許世賢傳奇/Chiayi's Heavenly Mother: The Romance of Hsu Shih-hsien]. Chiayi: Zhang jintong Xu Shixian jijinhui.

Chi Hsing [紀欣]. 2004. *"Yi guo liang zhi" zai Taiwan* [「一國兩制」在台灣/"One Country, Two Systems" in Taiwan]. Taipei: Haixia xueshu.

Chiang Kai-shek. 1968. "Dui quanguo da, zhong, xiaoxue zishen youliang jiaoshi zhici [對全國大、中、小學資深優良教師致詞/Address to the Distinguished Senior Faculty of the Nation's Universities, High Schools, and Primary Schools]." Republican year 57, September 28. "speeches/演講" folder, www.chungcheng.org.tw/thought/default.htm (accessed December 21, 2011).

"China Charter 08." 2009. Perry Link, trans. *New York Review of Books*, January 15, 54-56.

China Post. 2009. "Taiwan's Indigenous People up 2.05 percent." February 15. www.chinapost.com.tw/taiwan/national/national-news/2009/02/15/196128/Taiwan's-indigenous.htm (accessed April 19, 2012).

_____. 2012a. "Voters clearly in the mood for another four blue years," January 15. www.chinapost.com.tw/editorial/taiwan-issues/2012/01/15/329059/Voters-clearly.htm (accessed February 6, 2012).

_____. 2012b. "Will our parliament remain one of the worst in the world?" January 31. www.chinapost.com.tw/editorial/taiwan-issues/2012/01/31/330081/p2/Will-our.htm (accessed February 6, 2012).

China Realtime Report. 2011. "Taiwanese Students Resist Mandatory Confucian Studies." *China Digital Times.* http://chinadigitaltimes.net/2011/04/taiwanese-students-resist-mandatory-confucian-studies/ (accessed September 30, 2011).

Chiu Hei-Yuan [瞿海源]. 1997. *Taiwan zongjiao bianqian de shehui zhengzhi fenxi* [台灣宗教變遷的社會政治分析/A Socio-Political Analysis of Religious Change in Taiwan]. Taipei: Guiguan tushu.

Chou Bih-Er, Cal Clark, and Janet Clark. 1990. *Women in Taiwan Politics: Overcoming Barriers to Women's Participation in a Modernizing Society.* Boulder, CO: Lynne Rienner.

Chu Yun-han, Larry Diamond, Andrew J. Nathan, and Doh Chull Shin. 2008. *How East Asians View Democracy.* New York: Columbia University Press.

Chu Yun-han, and Lin Jih-wen. 2001. "Political Development in 20th-Century Taiwan: State-Building, Regime Transformation and the Construction of National Identity." Pp. 102-129 in Richard Louis Edmonds and Steven M. Goldstein, eds. *Taiwan in the Twentieth Century: A Retrospective View.* Cambridge: Cambridge University Press.

Chua, Beng-Huat. 1995. *Communitarian Ideology and Democracy in Singapore.* London: Routledge, 1995.

Chuang Ching-Sheng [莊景升]. 2006. "Dangdai renquan jiazhi yu rujia sixiang guanlian xing zhi yanjiu [當代人權價值與儒家思想關聯性之研究/Research on the Nature of Confucianism and Contemporary Human Rights Values]." M.A. thesis. Taipei: National Chengchi University.

Clower, Jason. 2010. *The Unlikely Buddhologist: Tiantai Buddhism in Mou Zongsan's New Confucianism.* Leiden: Brill.

Confucius. 1971 [ca. 500 B.C.E.]. *Confucian Analects, The Great Learning & The Doctrine of the Mean.* James Legge, trans. New York: Dover.

Copper, John F. 2003. *Taiwan: Nation-State or Province?* Boulder, CO: Westview Press.

Council for Cultural Affairs. 2011. "Publishing Act." *Encyclopedia of Taiwan.* http://taiwanpedia.culture.tw/en/content?ID=3967 (accessed January 17, 2012).

Council of Labor Affairs. 2005. "Gender Equality in Employment Act." http://laws.cla.gov.tw/eng/EngContent.asp?msgid=44 (accessed May 14, 2012).

Daily Mail. 2007. "Taiwan lawmakers brawl in parliament, again." *Mail Online,* May 8. www.dailymail.co.uk/news/article-453424/Taiwan-lawmakers-brawl-parliament-again.html (accessed March 9, 2012).

Davison, Gary Marvin, and Barbara E. Lee. 1998. *Culture and Customs of Taiwan.* Westport, CT: Greenwood Press.

de Bary, Wm. Theodore. 1998. *Asian Values and Human Rights.* Cambridge, MA: Harvard University Press.

Delury, John. 2007. "Harmonious in China." *Policy Review* 148(April-May): 35-44.

Department of Education. 1980. *Education in Taiwan Province.* Taipei: Department of Education.

Duncan, John B. 2002. "Uses of Confucianism in Modern Korea." Pp. 431-462 in Benjamin A. Elman, John B. Duncan, and Herman Ooms, eds. *Rethinking Confucianism: Past and Present in China, Japan, Korea, and Vietnam.* Los Angeles: UCLA Center for Chinese Studies.

Durdin, Tillman. 1947. "Formosa Killings Are Put at 10,000: Foreigners Say the Chinese Slaughtered Demonstrators Without Provocation." *New York Times,* March 29, 6.

Eckert, Carter J., Ki-baik Lee, Young Ick Lew, Michael Robinson, and Edward W. Wagner. 1990. *Korea Old and New: A History.* Cambridge, MA: Harvard University Korea Institute.

Education Ministry [Republic of China]. 1973. *Shehui: Guomin xiaoxue kecheng shi yanjiu baogao* [社會：國民小學課程實研究報告/Social Studies: A Reliable Research Report on Textbooks in Public Elementary Schools]. Taipei: Education Ministry.

Elman, Benjamin A., John B. Duncan, and Herman Ooms, eds. 2002. *Rethinking Confucianism: Past and Present in China, Japan, Korea, and Vietnam.* Los Angeles: UCLA Asia-Pacific Institute.

Elstein, David. 2010. "Why Early Confucianism Cannot Generate Democracy." *Dao* 9:427-443.

EVA Airways. 2005. "Employment." www.evaair.com/html/b2c/english/global_tools/carop/ (accessed Nov. 3, 2005).

Fan Ching-wen [范菁文]. 2007. "2007 nian Lianheguo tebie diaocha yuan baogao [2007 年聯合國特別調查員報告/2007 United Nations Members' Special Survey Report]." *Renquan zazhi* [人權雜誌/Human Rights Magazine] summer:10-13.

Fan, Maureen. 2007. "Confucius Making a Comeback in Money-Driven Modern China." *Washington Post Foreign Service,* July 24, A1.

Fan Yun [范雲]. 2004. "Xingbie yu shehui yundong [性別與社會運動/Gender and Social Movements]." *Nüxue xuezhi* [女學學誌/Journal of Women's and Gender Studies] 17:102-110.

Fetzer, Joel S., and J. Christopher Soper. 2007. "The Effect of Confucian Values on Support for Democracy and Human Rights in Taiwan," *Taiwan Journal of Democracy* 3(1):143-54.

_____. 2010. "Confucian Values and Elite Support for Liberal Democracy in Taiwan: The Perils of Priestly Religion." *Politics and Religion* 3(3):495-517.

Freedom House. 2008. "Taiwan 2008." *Freedom in the World, 2008.* www.freedomhouse.org/template.cfm?page=363&year=2008 (accessed February 6, 2009).

_____. 2009. *Freedom in the World, 2009.* www.freedomhouse.org/template.cfm?page=363&year=2009 (accessed May 25, 2010).

Freeman, Michael. 1995. "Human Rights: Asia and the West." Pp. 13-24 in James T. H. Tang, ed. *Human Rights and International Relations in the Asia-Pacific Region.* London: Pinter.

Fukuzawa Yukichi. 2008 [1875]. *An Outline of a Theory of Civilization.* David A. Dilwoth and G. Cameron Hurst III, trans. New York: Columbia University Press.

Geddes, Barbara. 2009. "What Causes Democratization?" Pp. 593-615 in Robert E. Goodin, ed. *Oxford Handbook of Political Science.* Oxford: Oxford University Press.

Glendon, Mary Ann. 1999. "Foundations of Human Rights: The Unfinished Business." *American Journal of Jurisprudence* 44 (2):1-14.

Gold, Thomas B. 1986. *State and Society in the Taiwan Miracle.* Armonk, NY: M. E. Sharpe.

_____. 1996. "Civil Society in Taiwan: The Confucian Dimension." Pp. 244-258 in Tu Wei-ming, ed. *Confucian Traditions in East Asian Modernity: Moral Education and Economic Culture in Japan and the Four Mini-Dragons.* Cambridge, MA: Harvard University Press.

Goldin. Paul R. 2011. *Confucianism.* Berkeley: University of California Press.

Gould, Andrew C. 1999. *Origins of Liberal Dominance: State, Church, & Party in Nineteenth-Century Europe.* Ann Arbor: University of Michigan Press.

Government Information Office. 2009. *The Republic of China Yearbook 2009.* Taipei: Government Information Office.

Gregor, A. James, and Maria Hsia Chang. 1979. "Anti-Confucianism: Mao's Last Campaign." *Asian Survey* 19(11):1073-1092.

He Baogang. 2004. "Confucianism Versus Liberalism over Minority Rights: A Critical Response to Will Kymlicka," *Journal of Chinese Philosophy* 31(1):103-123.

_____. 2010. "Four Models of the Relationship between Confucianism and Democracy." *Journal of Chinese Philosophy* 37(1):18-33.

Hill, Michael. 2000. "'Asian values' as reverse Orientalism: Singapore." *Asia Pacific Viewpoint* 41(2):177-190.

_____, and Lian Kwen Fee. 1995. *The Politics of Nation Building and Citizenship in Singapore.* London: Routledge.

Hong, Caroline. 2005a. "Law Protecting Aboriginal Rights is Praised." *Taipei Times,* January 22, 3.

_____. 2005b. "Lien, Hu share 'vision' for peace." *Taipei Times,* April 30, 1. www.taipeitimes.com/News/front/archives/2005/04/30/2003252532 (accessed October 26, 2011).

Hsu Chia-ching [徐佳青]. 2001. "Funü renquan [婦女人權/The Human Rights of Women]." Pp. 115-125 in Chen Chun-Hung [陳俊宏], ed. *Erqian nian zhi renquan zai Taiwan* [二千年之人權在台灣/Human Rights in Taiwan in the Year 2000]. Taipei: Taiwan Association for Human Rights.

Hu Shaohua. 1997. "Confucianism and Western Democracy." *Journal of Contemporary China* 6(15):347-363.

Huang, Chün-chieh, and Wu Kuang-ming. 1994. "Taiwan and the Confucian Aspiration: Toward the Twenty-First Century." Pp. 69-87 in Steven Harrell and Huang Chün-chieh, eds. *Cultural Change in Postwar Taiwan.* Boulder, CO: Westview.

Huntington, Samuel. 1996. *The Clash of Civilizations and the Remaking of World Order* New York: Simon and Schuster.

Hwang, Kwang-Kuo. 2001. "Introducing Human Rights Education in the Confucian Society of Taiwan: its Implications for Ethical Leadership in Education." *International Journal of Leadership in Education* 4(4):321-332.

Inglehart, Ronald. 1989. *Culture Shift in Advanced Industrial Society.* Princeton, New Jersey: Princeton University Press.

Jacobs, Andrew, Ian Johnson, Yang Xiyan, and Mia Lin. 2011. "Confucius Stood Here, But Not for Very Long." *New York Times,* April 23, A4.

Jacobsen, Michael, and Ole Bruun, eds. 2000. *Human Rights and Asian Values: Contesting National Identities and Cultural Representations in Asia.* Richmond, England: Curzon Press.

Jiang Qing. 2012. *A Confucian Constitutional Order: How China's Ancient Past Can Shape its Political Future.* Princeton: Princeton University Press.

_____, and Daniel A. Bell. 2012. "A Confucian Constitution for China." *New York Times,* July 10, A25.

Jochim, Christian. 2003. "Carrying Confucianism into the Modern World: The Taiwan Case." Pp. 48-83 in Philip Clart and Charles B. Jones, eds. *Religion in Modern Taiwan: Tradition and Innovation in a Changing Society.* Honolulu: University of Hawai'i Press.

Kalyvas, Stathis N. 1996. *The Rise of Christian Democracy in Europe.* Ithaca, NY: Cornell University Press.

Kerr, George H. 1965. *Formosa Betrayed.* Boston: Houghton Mifflin.

Kim Dae Jung. 1994. "Is Culture Destiny? The Myth of Asia's Anti-Democratic Values." *Foreign Affairs* 73(November-December). www.foreignaffairs.com/articles/50557/kim-dae-jung/is-culture-destiny-the-myth-of-asias-anti-democratic-values (accessed April 20, 2012).

Kim Kwang-ok. 1996. "The Reproduction of Confucian Culture in Contemporary Korea: An Anthropological Study." Pp. 202-227 in Tu Wei-ming, ed. *Confucian Traditions in East Asian Modernity: Moral Education and Economic Culture in Japan and the Four Mini-Dragons.* Cambridge, MA: Harvard University Press.

King, Ambrose Y.C. 1996. "State Confucianism and its Transformation: The Restructuring of the State-Society Relation in Taiwan." Pp. 228-243 in Tu Wei-ming, ed. *Confucian Traditions in East Asian Modernity: Moral Education and Economic Culture in Japan and the Four Mini-Dragons.* Cambridge, MA: Harvard University Press.

Ko Shu-ling. 2002. "Gender Equality Law Now a Reality." *Taipei Times,* March 7, 1.

Koh Byong-ik. 1996. "Confucianism in Contemporary Korea." Pp. 191-201 in Tu Wei-ming, ed. *Confucian Traditions in East Asian Modernity: Moral Education and Economic Culture in Japan and the Four Mini-Dragons.* Cambridge, MA: Harvard University Press.

Ku Kun-hui. 2005. "Rights to Recognition: Minority/Indigenous Politics in the Emerging Taiwanese Nationalism." *Social Analysis* 49(2):99-121.

Kung Wen-chi. 2000. *Indigenous People and the Press: A Study of Taiwan.* Taipei: Han-lu Publisher.

Kuo, Eddie C.Y. 1992. "Confucianism as Political Discourse in Singapore: The Case of An Incomplete Revitalization Movement." National University of Singapore Department of Sociology Working Paper no. 113. Singapore: National University of Singapore.

Lai Tse-han, Ramon H. Myers, and Wei Wou. 1991. *A Tragic Beginning: The Taiwan Uprising of February 28, 1947.* Stanford, CA: Stanford University Press.

Landler, Mark. 2000. "Man in the News; A Determined Fighter Who Paid a Price." *New York Times,* March 19.

Lee Kuan Yew. 2000. *From Third World to First, the Singapore Story: 1965-2000.* New York: Harper Collins.

Lee Ming-huei (李明輝). 2005. *Rujia shiye xia de zhengzhi sixiang* [儒家視野下的政治思想/Political Thought in the Light of Confucianism]. Taipei: National Taiwan University Press.

Lee Teng-hui [李登輝]. 1995. "Chinese Culture and Political Renewal." *Journal of Democracy* 6 (October):3-8.

_____. 2004. *Jianzheng Taiwan: Jiang Jingguo zongtong yu wo* [見證台灣：蔣經國總統與我/Eyewitness to Taiwan: President Chiang Ching-kuo and I]. Taipei: Yunchen wenhua.

Legislative Yuan Official Gazette [立法院公報]. 1988. January 13, vol. 77, period 4.

_____. 1998. November 7, vol. 87, period 45.

_____. 1999a. January 16, vol. 88, period 5, part 1 [上].

_____. 1999b. July 3, vol. 88, period 38.

_____. 2000. October 21, vol. 89, period 55, part 2 [下].

_____. 2004. November 15, vol. 93, period 44, part 1 [上].

Lele, Amod. 2004. "State Hindutva and Singapore Confucianism as Responses to the Decline of the Welfare State." *Asian Studies Review* 28(3):267-282.

Li Chenyang. 1997. "Confucian value and democratic value." *Journal of Value Inquiry* 31 (2):183-193.

Li Xiaofeng [李筱峰]. 2002. *Kuaidu Taiwan shi* [快讀台灣史/Summary History of Taiwan]. Taipei: Yushan.

Lieberman, Robert. 2002. "Ideas, Institutions, and Political Order: Explaining Political Change." *American Political Science Review* 96(4/December):697-712.

Lin Shu-Ya [林淑雅]. 2000. *Diyi minzu: Taiwan Yuanzhuminzu yundong de xianfa yiyi* [第一民族：台灣原住民族運動的憲法意義/First People: The Constitutional Meaning of the Indigenous Taiwanese Movement]. Taipei: Avanguard.

_____. 2001. "Yuanzhumin renquan baogao [原住民人權報告/Report on the Human Rights of Indigenous Peoples]." Pp. 127-137 in Chen Chun-Hung [陳俊宏], ed. *Erqian nian zhi renquan zai Taiwan* [二千年之人權在台灣/Human Rights in Taiwan in the Year 2000]. Taipei: Taiwan Association for Human Rights.

Lipset, Seymour Martin. 1959. "Some Social Requisites of Democracy: Economic Development and Political Legitimacy." *American Political Science Review* 53:69-105.

Liu Meihui. 2006. "Civics Education in Taiwan: Values Promoted in the Civics Curriculum." *Asia Pacific Journal of Education* 20(1):73-81.

Liu Xiang [劉向]. 2012 [ca. 15 B.C.E]. *Shuo Yuan* [說苑/Garden of Stories]. http://ctext.org/shuo-yuan/li-jie (accessed May 14, 2012).

Loa Iok-sin. 2009. "Watchdog still concerned about media interference." *Taipei Times,* December 19, 1.

Low, Y. F. 2012. "*Liberty Times*: An Ugly Farewell." January 21. http://focustaiwan.tw/ShowNews/WebNews_Detail.aspx?ID=201201210012&Type=aOPN (accessed February 6, 2012).

Lynch, Daniel C. 2006. *Rising China and Asian Democratization.* Stanford, CA: Stanford University Press.

Madsden, Richard. 2007. *Democracy's Dharma: Religious Renaissance and Political Development in Taiwan.* Berkeley: University of California Press.

Makeham, John. 2008. *Lost Soul: Confucianism in Contemporary Chinese Academic Discourse.* Cambridge, MA: Harvard University Press.

Marsh, Christopher. 2011. *Religion and the State in Russia and China: Suppression, Survival, and Revival.* New York: Continuum.

Mencius. 1970 [ca. 300 B.C.E.]. *The Mencius.* D.C. Lau, trans. Baltimore: Penguin Books.

Millan, Brandon Alexander, and Joel S. Fetzer. 2008. "Public Support for the 1990 Democracy Movement and Emigration from Taiwan: Exit *and* Voice or Exit *or* Voice?" *American Journal of Chinese Studies* 15(2):501-511.

Mona, Awi. 2007. "International Perspectives on the Constitutionality of Indigenous Peoples' Rights." *Taiwan International Studies Quarterly* 3(2):85-139.

Moody, Peter R., Jr. 1988. *Political Opposition in Post-Confucian Society.* New York: Praeger.

_____. 1996. "Asian Values." *Journal of International Affairs* 50(1):166-92.

Mooney, Paul. 2007. "Confucius Comes Back." *Chronicle of Higher Education*, April 20, 53(33):46.

Mou Zongsan [牟宗三]. 1968-1969. *Xinti yu xingti* [心體與性體/Mind and Human Nature]. 3 vols. Taipei: Zhengzhong shuju.

_____. 2003. *Spécificités de la philosophie chinoise.* Introduction by Joël Thoraval. Ivan P. Kamenarović and Jean-Claude Pastor, trans. Paris: Éditions du Cerf.

Nan Huai Chin [南懷瑾]. 2004. Lunyu biecai [論語別裁/A New Approach to the Confucian Analects], 5th ed. Hong Kong: Lao Ku Culture Foundation.

Nathan, Andrew J. 1993. "The Legislative Yuan Elections in Taiwan: Consequences of the Electoral System." *Asian Survey* 33(4/April):424-438.

_____, and Tse-hsin Chen. 2004. "Traditional Social Values, DemocraticValues, and Political Participation." Asian Barometer Working Paper No. 23. http://asianbarometer.org/newenglish/publications/workingpapers/no.23.pdf (accessed April 17, 2012).

NICT (National Institute for Compilation and Translation [國立編譯館]). 1960 [August, Republic of China year 49]. *Lishi keben* [歷史課本/History Textbook]. Elementary school, advanced level, first book, provisional edition. Taipei: National Institute for Compilation and Translation.

_____. 1965 [January, Republic of China year 54]. *Guoyu keben* [國語課本/Chinese Language Textbook]. Elementary school, beginning level, sixth book, provisional edition. Taipei: National Institute for Compilation and Translation.

_____. 1968a [January, Republic of China year 57]. *Shehui keben* [社會課本/Social Studies Textbook]. Elementary school, sixth grade, seventh book, provisional edition. Taipei: National Institute for Compilation and Translation.

_____. 1968b [January, Republic of China year 57]. *Shehui keben* [社會課本/Social Studies Textbook]. Elementary school, sixth grade, eighth book, provisional edition. Taipei: National Institute for Compilation and Translation.

_____. 2000 [August, Republic of China year 89]. *Shehui* [社會/Society]. Elementary school, sixth grade, eleventh book, seventh revised edition. Taipei: National Institute for Compilation and Translation.

_____. 2001 [August, Republic of China year 90]. *Guoyu* [國語/Chinese Language]. Elementary school, fourth grade, seventh book, first official edition. Taipei: National Institute for Compilation and Translation.

_____. 2002 [Republic of China year 91]. *Lishi jiaokeshu* [歷史教科書/History Textbook]. Middle school textbook, first book, second volume, third official edition. Taipei: National Institute for Compilation and Translation.

Nienhauser, William H. 1986. *The Indiana Companion to Traditional Chinese Literature.* Bloomington: Indiana University Press.

Noonan, John Thomas. 2005. *A Church that Can and Cannot Change: The Development of Catholic Moral Teaching.* South Bend, IN: University of Notre Dame Press.

Oldstone-Moore, Jennifer. 2003. *Understanding Confucianism.* London: Duncan Baird Publishers.

Pai Yi-Fong. 1995. "From Mainland to Island: The Transformation of the Elementary Social Studies Curriculum in Taiwan 1949-1993." Ph.D. dissertation. Madison: University of Wisconsin.

Park Chong Min and Doh Chull Shin. 2004. "Do Asian Values Deter Popular Support for Democracy? The Case of South Korea," Asian Barometer Working Paper No. 26. http://asianbarometer.org/newenglish/publications/workingpapers/no.26.pdf (accessed April 17, 2011).

Peng Ming-min. 1972. *A Taste of Freedom: Memoirs of a Formosan Independence Leader.* Upland, CA: Taiwan Publishing Co.

Pius IX. 2012 [1864]. "The Syllabus of Errors Condemned by Pius IX." *Papal Encyclicals Online.* www.papalencyclicals.net/Pius09/p9syll.htm (accessed April 13, 2012).

Przeworski, Adam, Michael E. Alvarez, José Antonio Cheibub, and Fernando Limongi. 2000. *Democracy and Development: Political Institutions and Well-Being in the World, 1950-1990.* Princeton: Princeton University Press.

Pye, Lucien. 2006. *Asian Power and Politics: The Cultural Dimensions of Authority* Cambridge, MA: Harvard University Press.

Rahim, Lily Zubaidah. 1998. *The Singapore Dilemma: The Political and Educational Marginality of the Malay Community.* Selangor Darul Ehsan, Malaysia: Oxford University Press.

Rigger, Shelley. 1984. "The Policy of the Republic of China toward Taiwan's Mountain People." Senior thesis. Woodrow Wilson School of Public and International Affairs, Princeton University.

_____. 1999. *Politics in Taiwan: Voting for Democracy.* London: Routledge.

_____. 2001. *From Opposition to Power: Taiwan's Democratic Progressive Party* Boulder, CO: Lynne Rienner Publishers.

Robinson, Michael. 1991. "Perceptions of Confucianism in Twentieth-Century Korea." Pp. 204-225 in Gilbert Rozman, ed. *The East Asian Region: Confucian Heritage and its Modern Adaptation.* Princeton: Princeton University Press.

Roy, Denny. 2003. *Taiwan: A Political History.* Ithaca, NY: Cornell University Press.

Rozman, Gilbert. 1991. "Comparisons of Modern Confucian Values in China and Japan." Pp. 157-203 in Gilbert Rozman, ed. *The East Asian Region: Confucian Heritage and its Modern Adaptation.* Princeton: Princeton University Press.

Rubinstein, Murray A. 2006. "The Presbyterian Church in the Formation of Taiwan's Democratic Society." Pp. 109-135 in Tun-jen Cheng and Deborah A. Brown, eds. *Religious Organizations and Democratization.* Armonk, NY: M. E. Sharpe.

Sansom, George. 1961. *A History of Japan 1334-1615.* Palo Alto: Stanford University Press.

Schirokauer, Conrad. 1991. *A Brief History of Chinese Civilization.* Stamford, CT: Thomson Learning.

Shih Ming-teh. 1998. "Taiwan." Pp. 5-61 in Chee Soon Juan, ed. *To be free: stories from Asia's struggle against oppression.* Clayton, Australia: Monash Asia Institute.

Shih Chia-yin [石佳音]. 2012. "Renmin tuanti fa [Civic Associations Act/人民團體法]." *Encyclopedia of Taiwan.* http://taiwanpedia.culture.tw/web/content?ID=100508& Keyword=非常時期人民團體組織法 (accessed March 9, 2012).

Shin Doh Chul, Myung Chey, and Kwang-Woong Kim. 1989. "Cultural Origins of Public Support for Democracy in Korea: An Empirical Test of the Douglas-Wildavsky Theory of Culture." *Comparative Political Studies* 22(2/July):217-238.

Shirk, Susan. 2007. *China, Fragile Superpower: How China's Internal Politics Could Derail Its Peaceful Rise.* Oxford: Oxford University Press.

Simon, Scott. 2010. "Negotiating Power: Elections and the constitution of indigenous Taiwan." *American Ethnologist* 37(4):726-740.

Slingerland, Edward G. 2008. "Classical Confucianism (I): Confucius and the *Lun-Yü.*" Pp. 107-136 in Bo Mou, ed. *Routledge History of Chinese Philosophy.* London: Routledge.

Smith, Rogers M. 1988. "Political Jurisprudence, the 'New Institutionalism,' and the Future of Public Law." *American Political Science Review* 82(1):89-108.

Song Young-Bae. 2002. "Crisis of Cultural Identity in East Asia: On the Meaning of Confucian Ethics in an Age of Globalization." *Asia Philosophy* 12(2):109-25.

Starr, Don. 2009. "Chinese Language Education in Europe: The Confucius Institutes." *European Journal of Education* 44(1):65-82.

Su Ya-Chen. 2006. "Political Ideology and Taiwanese School Curricula." *Asia Pacific Education Review* 7(1):41-50.

Taipei Times. 2009. "Editorial: KMT rolling back media freedom." February 6, 8.

_____. 2012. "Ma must turn to the economy." January 15. www.taipei-times.com/News/editorials/archives/2012/01/15/2003523242 (accessed February 6, 2012).

Taiwan Advocates [群策會]. 2003. *Taiwan 21 shiji guojia zongmubiao* [台灣 21 世紀國家總目標/Taiwan's National Agenda for the Twenty-First Century]. Taipei: Taiwan Advocates.

Tamney, Joseph B., and Linda Hsueh-Ling Chiang. 2002. *Modernization, Globalization, and Confucianism in Chinese Societies.* Westport, CT: Greenwood Press.

Tan Chwee Huat. 1989. "Confucianism and Nation Building in Singapore." *International Journal of Social Economics* 16(8):5-16.

Tan Yuan-ping (談遠平). 2004. *Zhongguo zhengzhi sixiang: rujia yu minzhuhua* [中國政治思想：儒家與民主化/Chinese Political Thought: Confucianism and Democratization]. Taipei: Yangzhi wenhua.

Taylor, Jay. 2000. *The Generalissimo's Son: Chiang Ching-kuo and the Revolutions in China and Taiwan.* Cambridge, MA: Harvard University Press.

_____. 2009. *The Generalissimo: Chiang Kai-shek and the Struggle for Modern China.* Cambridge, MA: Harvard University Press.

Thornberry, Milo L. 2011. *Fireproof Moth: A Missionary in Taiwan's White Terror.* Camp Hill, PA: Sunbury Press.

Tien Hung-Mao. 1989. *The Great Transition: Political and Social Change in the Republic of China.* Taipei: SMC Press.

Tocqueville, Alexis de. 1969 [1835]. *Democracy in America.* Garden City, New York: Anchor Books.

Tremewan, Christopher. 1996. *The Political Economy of Social Control in Singapore.* London: Macmillan.

Troeltsch, Ernst. 1960. *The Social Teachings of the Christian Churches.* New York: Harper and Row.

Tsai Ching-tien. 2002. "Chinese-ization and the Nationalistic Curriculum Reform in Taiwan." *Journal of Education Policy* 17(2):229-243.

United Nations. 1948. "The Universal Declaration of Human Rights." www.un.org/en/documents/udhr/ (accessed Oct. 27, 2011).

_____. 1979. "United Nations Convention on the Elimination of All Forms of Discrimination Against Women." www.un.org/womenwatch/daw/cedaw/text/e-convention.htm (accessed Oc. 27, 2011).

_____. 2008. "United Nations Declaration on the Rights of Indigenous Peoples." www.un.org/esa/socdev/unpfii/documents/DRIPS_en.pdf (accessed Oct. 27, 2011).

United Nations High Commission for Refugees. 2008. *World Directory of Minorities and Indigenous People—Taiwan.* www.unhcr.org/refworld/topic,463af2212,469f27b31-e0,49749c9fc,0,,COUNTRYREP,.html (accessed on February 28, 2012).

Vasil, Raj. 2004. *A Citizen's Guide to Government and Politics in Singapore.* Singapore: Talisman.

Wang Chien-chuan [王見川] and Li Shiwei [李世偉]. 1999. *Taiwan de zongjiao yu wenhua* [台灣的宗教與文化/Taiwan's Religion and Culture]. Taipei: BoyYoung.

Wang Fu-chang [王甫昌]. 2003. *Dangdai Taiwan shehui de zuqun xiangxiang* [當代台灣社會的族群想象/Ethnic Imagination in Contemporary Taiwan]. Taipei: Socio Publishing Co.

Wang Sheng. 1981. *The Thought of Dr. Sun Yat-sen.* Taipei: Li Ming Cultural Enterprise Co.

Wang Sung-Shan [王嵩山]. 2001. *Taiwan Yuanzhumin de shehui yu wenhua* [台灣原住民的社會與文化/Society and Culture of Indigenous Taiwanese]. Taipei: Lianjing.

Wang Ya-Ko [王雅各]. 1999. *Taiwan funü jiefang yundong shi* [台灣婦女解放運動史/History of the Taiwanese Women's Liberation Movement]. Taipei: Chuliu Publisher.

Wang Ying [王瑩], ed. 1994. *Yu lu gong wu: Taiwan Yuanzhumin wenhua (san)*[與鹿共舞:台灣原住民文化(三)/The Struggle for Renaissance: Taiwanese Indigenous Culture (III)]. Taipei: Sinorama Magazine.

Wang, Vincent Wei-cheng. 2007. "The Chinese Military and the 'Taiwan Issue': How China Assesses Its Security Environment." *Southeast Review of Asian Studies* 29:119-36.

Waltz, Susan. 2002. "Reclaiming and rebuilding the history of the Universal Declaration of Human Rights." *Third World Quarterly* 23(3):437-448.

Weatherly, Robert. 1999. *The Discourse of Human Rights in China.* London: Macmillan.

Weber, Max. 1951 [1915]. *The Religion of China: Confucianism and Taoism.* Hans H. Gerth, trans. Glencoe, IL: Free Press.

_____. 1958 [1905]. *The Protestant Ethic and the Spirit of Capitalism.* New York: Charles Scribner's Sons.

_____. 1963 [1922]. *The Sociology of Religion.* Boston: Beacon Press.

Wong, Edward. 2011. "Competing Confucius Award Bares Discord in China." *New York Times,* October 2, A8. www.nytimes.com/2011/10/02/world/asia/competing-confucius-award-bares-discord-in-china.html?ref=asia (accessed October 3, 2011).

Wong, John. 1996. "Promoting Confucianism for Socioeconomic Development: The Singapore Experience." Pp. 277-293 in Tu Wei-ming, ed. *Confucian Traditions in East Asian Modernity: Moral Education and Economic Culture in Japan and the Four Mini-Dragons.* Cambridge, MA: Harvard University Press.

Wright, Teresa. 2001. *The Perils of Protest: State Repression and Student Activism in China and Taiwan.* Honolulu: University of Hawai'i Press.

Wu, Tim E. M. 2005. *Minzhu DNA bijishu* [民主 DNA 筆記書/Notes of Democratic DNA]. Taipei: Third Nature Publishing Co.

Xu Fuguan [徐復觀]. 1979. *Rujia zhengzhi sixiang yu minzhu ziyou renquan* [儒家政治思想與民主自由人權/Confucian Political Thought and Democratic Freedom and Human Rights]. Taipei: Bashi niandai chubanshe.

_____, and Xiao Xinyi [蕭欣義]. 1988. *Rujia zhengzhi sixiang yu minzhu ziyou renquan* [儒家政治思想與民主自由人權/Confucian Political Thought and Democratic Freedom and Human Rights]. Taipei: Taiwan xuesheng shuju.

Yao Xinzhong. 2000. *An Introduction to Confucianism.* Cambridge: Cambridge University Press.

Zakaria, Fareed. 1994. "A Conversation with Lee Kuan Yew." *Foreign Affairs* 73(2):109-126.

Zhang Zuhua [张祖桦] et al. 2008. "Lingba xianzhang" [零八宪章/Charter 08]. On-line manifesto issued December 10. http://indymediacn.blogspot.com/2008/12/blog-post_10.html (accessed February 10, 2009).

Zhou Cezong. 1960. *The May Fourth Movement: Intellectual Revolution in Modern China.* Cambridge, MA: Harvard University Press.

Zimmermann, Christine. 1987. *Konfuziansimus und Feminismus in Taiwan: Lü Xiulian's Kampf für eine freie Gesellschaft.* Berlin: Verlag Ute Schiller.

Index

About the Authors

Joel S. Fetzer is Professor of Political Science at Pepperdine University in Malibu, California, and former Resident Director of the Pepperdine-in-China program in Hong Kong and Beijing. A graduate of Cornell and Yale Universities, he has also studied or served as visiting scholar at Georgetown University, the University of Southern California, the Taipei Language Institute, and the Chinese University of Hong Kong. His research and teaching primarily focus on immigration politics and on religion and politics in Western Europe, the United States, and East Asia. Professor Fetzer is the co-author (with J. Christopher Soper) of *Muslims and the State in Britain, France, and Germany.* A member of the editorial board of *Politics and Religion,* he has likewise published numerous articles in such academic journals as *International Migration Review, Journal of Ethnic and Migration Studies, Journal for the Scientific Study of Religion, American Journal of Chinese Studies,* and *Taiwan Journal of Democracy.*

    J. Christopher Soper is Distinguished Professor of Political Science at Pepperdine University. He received his Ph.D. from Yale University, his Master of Divinity from Yale Divinity School, and his B.A. from the University of Washington. Professor Soper is the author of *Religious Beliefs and Political Choices: Evangelical Christianity in the United States and Great Britain,* co-author (with Stephen Monsma) of *The Challenge of Pluralism: Church and State in Five Western Democracies* and *Faith, Hope, and Jobs: Welfare to Work in Los Angeles,* and co-author (with Joel S. Fetzer) of *Muslims and the State in Britain, France, and Germany.* Besides serving on the editorial board of *Journal for the Scientific Study of Religion*, Prof. Soper has contributed many articles to such publications as *Journal of Ethnic and Migration Studies, French Politics, Politics and Religion,* and *Taiwan Journal of Democracy.*